TOUR OF
THE VANOISE

In a region of such grand mountain architecture it is no wonder that Col de la Vanoise is so popular with walkers

TOUR OF
THE VANOISE

by

Kev Reynolds

CICERONE PRESS
MILNTHORPE, CUMBRIA, UK

© Kev Reynolds 1996
ISBN 1 85284 224 5
A catalogue record for this book is available from the British Library

ACKNOWLEDGEMENTS

My thanks to Andrew Harper for his welcome advice in the initial stages of research for this book. I am grateful, too, to Willi and Tim Meyer from Belgium, and to Hans, Ann, Jan and Eric de Bres from Holland who enlivened many evenings in huts along the way. To hut guardians for their smiles of welcome and on-the-spot route advice, to the staff of the region's tourist offices, to my publishers who were persuaded that this was a route worthy of a guidebook, to Rosemary Durose for help with translations, and most of all, to my wife who walked the trails with me, patiently served as a figure in the landscape for my photographs, and who is the best of all companions - both in the mountains and at home. Sincere thanks to them all.

Kev Reynolds

Cicerone guides by the same author:

Walks in the Engadine - Switzerland
The Valais
The Bernese Alps
Ticino - Switzerland
Central Switzerland
The Jura (with R.B. Evans)
Alpine Pass Route
Chamonix to Zermatt - the Walker's Haute Route
Annapurna - a Trekker's Guide
Everest - a Trekker's Guide
Langtang, Gosainkund & Helambu - a Trekker's Guide
Walking in Kent Vols I & II
The Wealdway & The Vanguard Way
The South Downs Way & The Downs Link
The Cotswold Way
Walks & Climbs in the Pyrenees

Cover: Pt. de Bellecôte and Plan d'Aval

CONTENTS

Introduction 8

    The Vanoise National Park 10

    Getting There 13

    When to Go 14

    Accommodation. 15

    Maps & Waymarks... 18

    Preparations & Equipment 18

    Safety in the Mountains 21

    Using the Guide 23

The Route 26

Stage 1: Modane - Refuge de l'Orgère 26

Stage 2: Refuge de l'Orgère - Col du Barbier - Refuge du
               Plan Sec 32

Stage 3: Refuge du Plan Sec - Refuge de l'Arpont 37

Stage 4: Refuge de l'Arpont - Refuge du Plan du Lac 43

Stage 5: Refuge du Plan du Lac - Refuge du Vallonbrun 50

Stage 6: Refuge du Vallonbrun - Bonneval-sur-Arc 56

Stage 7: Bonneval-sur-Arc - Col de l'Iseran - Val d'Isère 62

Stage 8: Val d'Isère - Col de la Leisse - Refuge de la Leisse 68

Stage 9: Refuge de la Leisse - Col de la Vanoise - Pralognan 74

Alternative Stage 9: Refuge de la Leisse - Refuge d'Entre
               Deux Eaux - Refuge de la Femma - Refuge d'Entre
               Deux Eaux 82

Stage 10: Pralognan - Refuge de Péclet-Polset 85

Stage 11: Refuge de Péclet-Polset - Col de Chavière - Modane .. 90

Route Summary 95

Short Tours in the Vanoise 96

    Tour des Glaciers de la Vanoise 96

    Tour of the Eastern Vanoise 98

    Traverse of the Vanoise 99

Appendices

    A: Useful Addresses 101

    B: Refuge Reservation 103

    C: Bibliography 105

    D: Metric Conversions 107

    E: Glossary 109

ADVICE TO READERS

Readers are advised that whilst every effort is taken by the author to ensure the accuracy of this guidebook, changes can occur which may affect the contents. It is advisable to check locally on transport, accommodation, shops, etc. but even rights of way can be altered and, more especially overseas, paths can be eradicated by landslip, forest fires or changes of ownership.

    The publisher would welcome notes of any such changes.

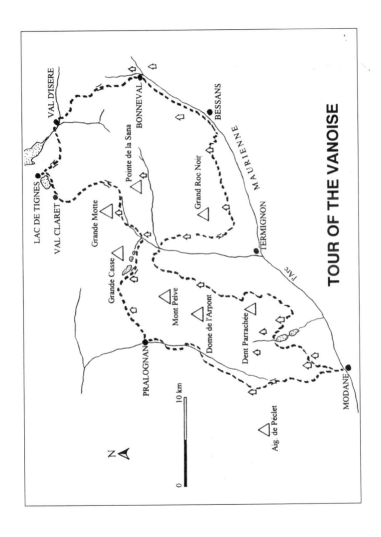

TOUR OF THE VANOISE

Introduction

This book is a guide to a 10-12 day walking tour of one of the most attractive mountain regions of France. The Vanoise Alps, wedged between Mont Blanc and the Massif des Écrins, provide not only a magnificent backdrop of 3000 metre (10,000ft) peaks, but an array of glaciers and snowfields, gleaming tarns, streams and waterfalls, beautiful alpine meadows flushed with an amazing kaleidoscope of wild flowers, isolated farms and tiny hamlets that belong, it seems, to an age long forgotten, a scattering of mountain huts, old stone ruins and abundant wildlife - it would be a very unobservant walker indeed who could complete the Tour of the Vanoise without noting at least marmots, chamois and bouquetin (*ibex*) from the trail.

The tour explores the very best of the Vanoise National Park and should appeal to all keen mountain walkers. Covering a distance of more than 154 kilometres (95 miles) it encounters some dramatic wild landscapes, is demanding in places and, with several passes to tackle in excess of 2500 metres (8200ft), ensures there's plenty of height gain and loss; the total amount of ascent being some 7031 metres (23,068ft). Each stage has its challenge and its rewards. But there are no glacier crossings, no scrambling sections, no lengthy paths exposed to either stonefall or vertigo-inspiring exposure. Waymarks and cairns are mostly sufficient guides where the trail is indistinct, and in places signposts have been erected that provide a rough indication of the time required to reach the next hut, col or village along the way.

The route is an obvious one. By combining sections of that classic long-distance trail, the GR5 (*La Grande Traversée des Alpes*) on its way from Lake Geneva to the Mediterranean, with the GR55 which cuts through the heart of the region, a neat, almost-figure-of-eight, tour becomes practicable. A shorter tour, dealing with the western loop below the Glaciers de la Vanoise, has become popular with French walkers to whom it is known as the *Tour des Glaciers de la Vanoise*; there's also the possibility of creating a circuit of the eastern Vanoise in less than a week, while the five-day traverse of the range from Landry in the Tarentaise to Modane in the Arc valley has plenty of advocates too. But it is this convoluted tour that provides the greatest variety of scenic pleasures and the most rewards; a trek that deserves to become a classic in its own right.

Beginning in Modane in the Maurienne (the valley of the River Arc), the GR5 climbs steeply through forest to the edge of the National Park, then contours north-eastward to a deeply-cut glen containing two dammed lakes and a choice of three mountain huts on the southern flank of an extensive mountain mass bearing the largest glacier complex of the region. From Plan Sec an undulating trail crosses a mountain spur, then turns roughly northward on a long but spectacular diversion above the narrow Doron gorge. At the gorge's northern limit the way descends to green pastures, then curves southward, climbing to a gentle, high plateau with glorious views across the unseen gorge to the Glaciers de la Vanoise slung between La Dent Parrachée and Pointe de la Réchasse.

Continuing south raw mountain scenery is exchanged for a more pastoral landscape. Then the path breaks out of the Doron valley and heads eastward, high above the Haute-Maurienne with steep meadows hanging from mid-mountain slopes. Refuge du Vallonbrun nestles in a quiet, secretive, glen-like terrace opposite the glaciers of Pointe de Ronce which guards the international road pass of Col du Mont Cenis. That road is but a distant twisting line, but beyond Vallonbrun the tour descends sharply to Col de la Madeleine and the Haute-Maurienne where traffic labours on its way to the Col de l'Iseran, second highest col in the French Alps after Col de la Bonette. The walker's route through Haute-Maurienne, however, is loud with crickets, not traffic, as the path wades through fragrant meadows and patches of woodland, by-passes Bessans and continues in the bed of the valley to Bonneval-sur-Arc, a charming, medieval stone-built village that actively shuns all external signs of modernity. (An alternative high trail climbs beyond Bessans and rejoins the other route north of Bonneval.)

Between timeless Bonneval and the modern sophistication of Val d'Isère, the route crosses Col de l'Iseran (2764m: 9068ft), but does so by way of a delightful approach through the Vallon de la Lenta. Descent to Val d'Isère temporarily leaves the National Park, although

9

for a while it goes through a nature reserve, samples some of France's most popular and challenging ski terrain, and returns to the haven of the park south-east of Tignes where GR55 is joined. The crossing of Col de la Leisse in the shadow of La Grande Motte leads into the U-shaped scoop of Vallon de la Leisse flanked by the great wall that links La Grande Motte with La Grande Casse, the latter being the highest peak in the Vanoise Alps at 3855 metres (12,648ft). Refuge de la Leisse is set mid-way through the valley, and it is an easy day's walk from there to reach either Refuge du Col de la Vanoise or the little resort town of Pralognan-la-Vanoise, while an alternative option is to stray southward to Entre Deux Eaux and the Vallon de la Rocheure before returning to the tour proper and crossing Col de la Vanoise.

The final stretch, either tackled as a very long day or two more acceptable stages, follows the Chavière torrent upstream along the fringe of the National Park to Refuge de Péclet-Polset, and a crossing of the highest pass tackled by any GR (*Grande Randonnée*) route, Col de Chavière (2796m: 9173ft) by which the Maurienne is regained at Modane.

THE VANOISE NATIONAL PARK

Situated between the upper valleys of the Isère (Tarentaise) and Arc (Maurienne) in the *département* of Savoie, and adjoining Italy's Gran Paradiso National Park along a 14 kilometre (9 mile) common boundary, the *Parc National de la Vanoise* (PNV) was established in 1963 - the first in France. The two parks were twinned in 1972, and together they constitute the largest nature reserve in western Europe.

The PNV covers an area of 53,000 hectares (205 sq miles) of high mountains and deep, verdant valleys, ranging in altitude from 1250 to 3855 metres (4101-12,648ft). There are 107 peaks over 3000 metres (9843ft) high, and a network of around 500 kilometres (310 miles) of footpaths, many of which are snow-free from mid June to late October. Within the central and peripheral zones there are 42 refuges totalling more than 1900 beds. Nineteen of these refuges belong to the park authority, 12 are owned by the CAF (*Club Alpin Français*) and 11 are in private ownership.

While tourist development, especially downhill skiing, has been encouraged on the park's periphery, the central zone is protected from outside exploitation, and despite a small amount of summer farms, there's no permanent habitation. As a result the park boasts an abundance of wildlife, including some 700 bouquetin, which represents half the population in France, and about 4500 chamois. In addition walkers following the Tour of the Vanoise will frequently hear and see marmots, stand a good chance of observing ermine, common lizards and, possibly, the mountain hare, while ornithologists can train their binoculars on an assortment of bird-life ranging from the ptarmigan and three-toed woodpecker, to the golden eagle and recently reintroduced lammergeier.

For most walkers a sighting of bouquetin will be the greatest prize. These short-legged, stocky animals live and graze in herds; mostly the sexes remaining apart until the rut when one proud buck may win a harem of females. The male sports a large and majestic pair of knobbly, scimitar-shaped horns that are used in battle with rival males during the autumn rut. The female's horns are much shorter. In the 19th century the bouquetin was extinct in almost every part of the European Alps, with the exception of the Gran Paradiso where it was protected. Gradually small herds were reintroduced to other Alpine regions, and it was partly in an attempt to protect those of the Vanoise massif that the PNV was established. Bouquetin can often be seen grazing quite close to Refuge de l'Arpont.

Chamois are extremely agile creatures that also move around the high mountains in small herds, although solitary males are not at all uncommon. Shy and suspicious of man, they roam the screes and remote pastures just below the snowline. With short, curved horns they are sometimes mistaken for female, or young, bouquetin - especially when viewed from a distance. They are, however, more streamlined and with longer legs than the bouquetin.

The most engaging of all mountain creatures is the marmot, a brown, furry mammal that lives in burrows in the high pastures or boulder-strewn slopes. Growing to the size of a large hare, the marmot hibernates in winter for as much as six months until the snow cover melts. Young are born in the early summer, and it's not unusual to spy three or four kitten-like creatures playing in the warm sunshine, or nibbling the succulent grasses. Often the first indication of a nearby marmot colony is a high shrill whistle - a warning cry. Follow

11

the sound and you will probably see one or more of these creatures sitting upright and surveying the immediate surroundings for sign of danger. On every stage of this walk there will be opportunities to study marmots from the trail.

As for mountain flowers, above 1500 metres (4900ft) in the central and peripheral zones, more than 1000 species have been noted. Not only Alpine natives, but southern and oriental species too, and Arctic-Alpines left behind by previous ice ages. The trekker following trails described in this guidebook will be reminded daily of the richness of this flora. Much depends, of course, on the timing of one's visit, but there will always be something worth noting almost from the moment the snows start to recede, right through to the autumn. The most extensive display will be found in late June or early July, when every level - from deep valley to high pass - will be extravagant with colour.

Valley meadows between Col de la Madeleine (below Refuge du Vallonbrun) and Bonneval are among the most lavish, as to flora, in all the Vanoise. Go there in early summer and you'll be wading through swamps of orchid, polygonum, dianthus, larkspur and vetch. There'll be cowslip, marsh marigold, potentilla and yellow archangel, pink cranesbill and rockrose, vivid blue campanula, violas in assorted varieties and masses of clover thick with bees.

On sunny hillsides up to 2000 metres (6562ft) or more the lovely delicate white blooms of St Bruno's lily (*Paradisea liliastrum*) will be seen in huge swathes, their several heads on a long stem all facing the same way. On other hillsides it might be the hairy-stemmed spring anemone (*Pulsatilla vernalis*) that dominates; or maybe its cousin, the white alpine anemone (*Pulsatilla alpina*).

In the shade of woods, on open pastures and in marshy places, the great yellow gentian (*Gentiana lutea*) - which looks nothing like either of the better-known spring, or trumpet, gentians - produces numerous flower clusters on an erect stalk that can be more than a metre (3ft) tall. The almost stemless *Gentiana verna* (spring gentian) appears all over the Vanoise, as does the aptly-named trumpet gentian (*Gentiana kochiana*), often found among soft pink primulas. Edelweiss grow near the Refuge de la Leisse, while those harbingers of spring, the tassle-headed soldanella, seemingly cannot wait for summer and will often be found blooming in the midst of a melting patch of late-winter snow.

Alpenroses form a great splash of scarlet on hillsides and in valleys throughout the Tour of the Vanoise; one of the finest displays being seen just above Pont de Croé-Vie on the eastern approach to Col de la Vanoise. Much smaller, but spreading as bright cushions on rocks, are assorted species of saxifrage and androsace, while the common houseleek (*Sempervivum tectorum*) - and other varieties - sprouts luxuriant flower stems in July from a fleshy rosette anchored to a wayside boulder.

Walkers eager to learn more about the plants likely to be found on their tour are directed to *The Alpine Flowers of Britain and Europe* by Christopher Grey-Wilson and Marjorie Blamey (Collins), or *Mountain Flowers* by Anthony Huxley (Blandford Press).

Visitors to the National Park must comply with a set of regulations, summarised by the following list, most of which will be second-nature to the majority of mountain walkers using this guide.

* Keep to paths and avoid creating short-cuts across hairpin bends.

* Do not pick flowers or wild fruits or collect rock samples. When photographing flowers please avoid damaging nearby vegetation.

* Make no unnecessary noise - no radios etc.

* Dogs are not allowed within the park, even on a lead.

* Leave no litter, and take rubbish away with you for proper disposal.

* Wild camping is forbidden, but lightweight tents are allowed in the vicinity of certain refuges, for which a fee is charged.

* Do not light fires.

* Hang-gliders and parapentes are forbidden in the park, as are mountain bikes.

GETTING THERE

By air:

Chambéry and Grenoble are the nearest airports to the Vanoise region, but as there are no direct flights from the UK connections will need to be made via Paris (Charles de Gaulle). However, direct flights

13

exist between London (Gatwick) and Lyon (Satolas), and are operated by British Airways. From Lyon take the train to Chambéry and on to Modane.

By rail:

The fastest approach by rail is via the TGV from Paris to Lyon, and change there for Chambéry and Modane. The alternative direct Paris-Turin service calls at Modane and will save changing trains.

By road:

The cheapest public transport route is by the Eurolines express coach service, which leaves London (Victoria) mid-afternoon and arrives in Chambéry the following morning in time for breakfast. From Chambéry take the train to Modane. (Bookings for this coach can be made through National Express agents, or in person at Eurolines, 52 Grosvenor Gardens, Victoria, London SW1. For telephone enquiries dial 01582 404511. BMC members can purchase tickets at the Youth rate via the BMC office.)

Travel by private car is not very satisfactory since the vehicle will need to be left unattended for the duration of the trek. But for those eager to travel this way, a fast motorway network through France leads almost unbroken from Calais to Chambéry. Note, however, that these motorways (*autoroutes*) are toll roads, and a journey of this length can become rather expensive as a result. Beware of travelling at weekends between mid-July and mid-August, and especially on 15 August (the Feast of the Assumption) which is a national holiday and French roads as a consequence are notoriously busy.

WHEN TO GO

The Vanoise region receives plenty of snowfall in winter - as evidenced by the existence of some of France's most popular ski slopes on the outer fringe of the National Park. The departure of this snow from the high cols determines the best time to tackle the tour, and although it may be possible to cross some of the passes as early as mid-June following a particularly mild winter season, the beginning of July is usually early enough - and even then some of the cols and north (or east) facing slopes can have their troublesome sections. Research for this guide was undertaken during July 1995 in the wake of extremely heavy snowfall in the spring of that year. Some stages were rather 'entertaining' as a result.

During June and July the wild flowers are at their best and meadows, as yet uncut, will reward with a most extravagant display of colour and fragrance, and thus provide one of the highlights of the region.

French holidays extend between mid-July and mid-August, and as huts are likely to be crowded during this period and, in extreme cases, fully booked, accommodation can be difficult to find unless pre-booked. August can be very warm. Protected by the Pre-Alps from oceanic rains, the massif enjoys a dry, sunny climate, almost Mediterranean in its intensity.

September offers, perhaps, the most favourable conditions for a walking tour of the Vanoise Alps. Gone are the crowds, summer's heat is beginning to wane and prolonged periods of settled weather are often to be had. Days, of course, are drawing in, but there should still be plenty of daylight in which to complete each stage. Although the best of the flowers will be over, the meadows and grassy hillsides still produce occasional gems.

ACCOMMODATION

Accommodation for walkers tackling the Tour of the Vanoise will mostly be in the form of mountain huts (*refuges*), of which there is a plentiful supply. As mentioned above, most of these have been constructed on behalf of the National Park authority, but there are also several in the care of the CAF, and others that are privately owned. There's very little difference in the cost of meals and beds in privately-run, CAF or PNV refuges. Membership of either the Friends of the National Park (*Amis du Parc National de la Vanoise*) or CAF will however result in a reduction in overnight fees, but such membership is not essential to secure a bed for the night. (Members of other Alpine Clubs with reciprocal rights - ie: holders of a UK membership card of the Austrian Alpine Club - can also claim a part-reduction in fees in CAF huts.)

Refuges provide basic facilities: communal washrooms and toilets, dining room and dormitory-style sleeping arrangements. In dormitories there's no segregation of the sexes. In some huts youth hostel style bunk beds are provided, but in others a large communal sleeping platform is the norm, where mattresses are laid out side by side, with a standard allocation of a single pillow and two blankets each. For comfort and hygiene a cotton sleeping bag liner (sheet sleeping bag) should be used, although there is no insistence on this.

The majority of refuges in the Vanoise region have a guardian in summer residence, and it is often his, or her, personality that helps create each hut's definable character. The guardian will allocate bedspace, and usually provide filling meals at set times. It is not usually necessary for individuals to book these in advance of arrival at the hut. Most huts (and those with no resident guardian) have a small kitchen with gas rings, pots and pans, crockery and cutlery, for use (for a small fee) by walkers who prefer to cater for themselves. Note, however, that self-caterers will need to provide all their own food.

On arrival at a refuge, walkers should remove their boots and leave them on a rack in the boot room or porch, and use the plastic hut shoes provided. Seek out the guardian, ask for a bed and order meals if required. The standard arrangement is for *demi pension* (evening meal and breakfast). Lunch packets may also be on offer if ordered the night before you leave. Once bedspace has been allocated (usually a specific numbered space) it is advisable to make your bed with your sheet sleeping bag while there's still light to see what you're doing, as some dormitories have no form of illumination other than that which comes through the window. Make sure you have a torch handy.

Evening meals prepared by the guardian will invariably consist of three or more courses, often with several helpings of soup and bread available. A simple meat course, served with either potatoes, rice or pasta, is often followed by a green salad, then cheese or choice of dessert. Wine, beer and soft drinks are sometimes on sale, as are tea, coffee and hot chocolate. Breakfasts are 'continental style' - plenty of bread and jam (sometimes cheese) and occasionally cereals. A choice of coffee, tea or hot chocolate will be offered.

Payment for your stay is usually, though not always, expected during the evening after dinner has been served. This is especially

Pierre Brune, a stone chalet set amid flower meadows on the approach to Refuge de l'Orgère
Pastures at Col du Barbier

Wayside pool above the Doron gorge en route to Refuge de l'Arpont
La Grande Casse (left) and la Grande Motte dominate the route north of
l'Arpont

important for those eager to make an early start in the morning.

The majority of refuges have a 'winter room' that is permanently open, where walkers can have use of a kitchen, sleeping room and toilet. This is particularly useful during those times of year when the guardian is not in residence and the main part of the hut is locked.

As already mentioned huts in the Vanoise National Park can be extremely busy during the period mid-July (14 July is Bastille Day) to mid-August, and it is not unusual to find all their beds booked. Should you plan to tackle the Tour of the Vanoise during this period, you are strongly recommended to make reservations in advance. Bookings for July and August can be made by post through a special central reservations facility organised by the tourist office in Pralognan. Details of this service, plus a sample letter in French, and the address to write to, will be found under Appendix B. (There is a per-person charge for this service.) The National Park receptionist at other tourist offices on the edge of the park (Modane, Bonneval, Val d'Isère) can also make reservations on your behalf if you make your request in person once you arrive in the area. Alternatively, for those who can confidently speak in French, it's possible to book via recorded telephone message. After dialling 04 36 68 71 49 you will hear a 'welcome message' after which you use either number keys or the star key on your phone to select the service you require: 'park information', 'accommodation reservation' - or 'leave a message'. In addition, most guardians will be happy to phone ahead on your behalf to book the next night's lodging at huts along the way. (Under details given for each hut along the tour mentioned in this guide, telephone numbers are provided.)

As a general rule wild camping is forbidden within the National Park, but lightweight tents are permitted (for a small fee) within the vicinity of the following huts on the tour: Refuge de l'Aiguille Doran, Refuge du Fond d'Aussois, Refuge de la Dent Parrachée, Refuge de l'Arpont, Refuge du Vallonbrun, Refuge de la Leisse, Refuge de la Femma. The stipulation is for small, lightweight tents on a transitory overnight basis only, between 7.00pm and 7.00am. Official campsites exist outside the park's boundaries at Modane, Bessans, Val d'Isère and Pralognan-la-Vanoise.

Most villages and towns on the route offer beds at a range of prices in hotels, pensions and, in some instances, *gîtes d'étape*, and where they exist mention is made in the main body of text. Lower-priced hotels are named in those places where a wide range of accommodation is available. For additional addresses, contact the local tourist office.

Gîtes d'étape are located throughout France along popular long-distance walking routes, and are rather like private youth hostels. (Do not confuse a *gîte d'étape* with a *Gîte de France*, for the latter is a cottage available for holiday let.) Like mountain refuges, *gîtes d'étape* provide basic facilities for an overnight stay, almost exclusively for walkers. Sleeping arrangements are usually bunk beds in dormitories, washrooms mostly have showers, and a well-equipped kitchen for self-catering is standard. As in refuges, the guardian often provides meals.

MAPS & WAYMARKS

The whole route is covered by an excellent map published by Editions Didier & Richard of Grenoble. In the series, Randonnées pédestres et à ski, *Massif et Parc National de la Vanoise* (sheet 11) at a scale of 1:50,000 is a reproduction of the IGN (*Institut Géographique National*) survey, with the main walking routes overprinted in blue, and refuges and *gîtes* highlighted in red. Sufficient detail is given at this scale to make the sheet perfectly adequate for step-by-step use along the trail, especially when used in conjunction with the present guidebook. It comes into its own in the planning stage at home, and will enable you to identify landmarks along the way. It is usually kept in stock at Stanfords in London, or should be available from shops in Modane.

Since the tour follows large sections of both GR5 and GR55 the standard waymark to look for is red and white horizontal stripes painted on trees, rocks or buildings. On occasion local walking tours adopt sections of the route, and then additional coloured stripes may also be seen. Hopefully these will not add too much confusion, and route descriptions in this book should keep you on course.

PREPARATIONS & EQUIPMENT

The Tour of the Vanoise may not be the most taxing route in the Alps, but it is certainly demanding enough. In fact the very first short stage out of Modane offers no gentle easing in. On the contrary, it is quite brutal in places as the trail climbs steeply out of the valley en route to Refuge de l'Orgère. Walkers who have done nothing to physically prepare themselves for such a start will regret the omission long before the hut comes in sight. Taking regular exercise at home will help; swimming, cycling, jogging are all useful, but the best possible preparatory exercise in advance of a walking tour is - walking. Uphill. As often as possible. Pack a small rucksack to take with you in order to accustom your shoulders to carrying weights, and find some hills to walk up. Once you set out from Modane on a warm summer's day, you'll be thankful you made an effort to get fit for the mountains.

In order to derive the maximum enjoyment from the tour it will not only be important to set out fit and eager, but to have the right clothing and equipment. Bear in mind that you will be heading into a high mountain environment, remote in places, and with the possibility of extreme weather conditions (even in mid-summer), and choose clothing that is not only functional and hard-wearing, but comfortable too. The following suggestions and check-list may be of some help in deciding what to take.

Boots with thick cleated soles (*Vibram* or similar) need to fit well and be comfortable. There will be a few stream crossings and snow patches to contend with, so footwear should be fairly waterproof, and with screes and occasional rough sections on descent, you will certainly require ankle support.

Gaiters can be useful when dealing with early-season snowfields or meadows after rain. Short ankle-cuffs (*stop tous*) are a good alternative.

Waterproofs are essential. A cagoule and overtrousers made of Gore-Tex, or other 'breathable' materials, are recommended, as is a warm pullover or medium-weight fleece jacket for evening wear and when resting on a high pass. A wool hat and gloves should also be taken in the event of cold conditions that may occur at any time.

So much for cold- and wet-weather gear. Summers in the Vanoise can prove very warm, so you will need protection from too much sun. A wide-brimmed hat will provide much-needed shade for neck and ears. Sunglasses are a must, as are high factor suncream and lip salve. Shorts are popular, but ensure you use plenty of suncream on exposed legs.

Unless your plans include camping you will not need a sleeping bag, other than a cotton sleeping bag liner for use in huts. A first aid kit is essential. Water bottle, guidebook, map, compass, whistle, headtorch (plus spare bulb and batteries) should also be carried, as should emergency food (bar of chocolate or similar). A camera and plenty of films will help record your tour.

Trekking poles have been used for a couple of decades or more by mountain walkers on the Continent, and are now gaining in popularity among trekkers from Britain. Having been 'converted' to their use in the Himalaya, I would be loath to undertake any wild-country trek now without one. For the uninitiated, a trekking pole is a lightweight telescopic ski stick which, when used properly, can relieve pressure on knees, aid balance when crossing streams, provide assistance and generate confidence when tackling snowfields or traversing steep hillsides, reduce leg-strain on sharp descents, and be of enormous benefit when carrying a heavy load. I would thoroughly recommend all walkers tackling the Tour of the Vanoise to use a trekking pole.

Finally, a well-fitting rucksack with a waist-belt correctly adjusted to take the weight of the pack is very important. It need not be a large sack, since all but the camper should be able to keep weight down to around 10 kilograms (22lbs). A fitted nylon rucksack cover is very useful when caught out in heavy rain. Pack all items in a thick polythene bag inside the sack as additional protection against wet weather. A 'survival bag' is useful in this respect. If needed in an emergency it can quickly be emptied of its contents.

Check-list:

Rucksack (plus cover & survival bag)	Cagoule
Boots (plus spare laces & cleaning kit)	Overtrousers
Gaiters (or *stop tous*)	Trousers (not jeans)
Shirts (x 3)	Shorts
Pullover (or fleece)	Underwear
Socks (x 3)	Wool hat
Gloves	Sunhat, sunglasses, suncream &
Sheet sleeping bag	lip salve
Headtorch (plus spare bulb &	Water bottle
batteries)	Toilet kit (plus small towel)
First aid	Mending kit

Toilet paper (plus lighter to burn same if caught out during the day)	Whistle
	Map & compass
Penknife	Guidebook
Camera & films (plus spare batteries)	Passport
Trekking pole	Travel tickets & insurance
Emergency food	documents

SAFETY IN THE MOUNTAINS

All who follow the routes described in this book should assume responsibility for their own safety, and look to the needs of those with them.

Most of the Tour of the Vanoise will be walked on clear, well-marked trails. But some stages lead through lonely, wild and seemingly desolate terrain where paths are sketchy and the route defined only by a line of cairns. There are some high passes to cross, streams to negotiate which, at certain times of the year, may be raging torrents that have swept away footbridges or submerged mild-season stepping stones. Such uncertainties add a piquant quality to a tour such as this, but they can also increase the possibility of accident. Natural hazards abound in mountain country, and all walkers should be aware of this and be prepared to cope with any that arise.

Plan each day's walk with care. Read the route descriptions in advance of setting out, and match them against the map until you have a mental picture of the day's journey, having particular regard to the amount of height gain and loss and estimated time it will take to reach the next hut. Note, also, any possible shelter along the trail that could be useful in the event of bad weather closing in. Check the weather forecast (refuge guardians usually pin a weather bulletin on their noticeboard each day), ensure you have sufficient food and liquid with you for the day ahead, and keep your first aid kit near at hand.

Know how to read the map and compass, do not overestimate your physical ability and bear in mind the limitations of the weakest or least-experienced member of the party. Be vigilant for anyone who might be showing signs of fatigue or the onset of illness. Never be too proud to turn back should it be safer to do so than to continue in the face of an on-coming storm, or other conditions that appear dangerous.

21

In the unhappy event of an accident, stay calm, administer first aid where applicable, and make the victim as warm and comfortable as possible, ensuring that he/she is in no immediate danger from rockfall or avalanche. Should your party be numerically large enough to send for help whilst someone remains with the injured member (it is better and safer to send two, rather than just one person for assistance), make a careful *written* note of the precise location where the victim can be found. Should a manned refuge be nearer, inform the guardian who will alert the rescue services, but if it is quicker to reach a village, inform the gendarmerie.

The international distress call is a series of six signals (blasts on a whistle, or torch flashes after dark) spaced evenly for a minute, followed by a minute's pause, then repeat with a further six signals. The recognised reply is three signals per minute followed by a minute's pause.

It is worth pointing out that there is no free mountain rescue service in the Alps, and that an emergency can therefore be extremely costly for the victim, his family or friends. Insurance that includes emergency mountain rescue is advisable. Ordinary holiday insurance will *not* include mountain rescue cover, and often standard holiday cover excludes persons engaged in mountaineering pursuits - check the small print. Specialist policies are available from:-

West Mercia Insurance Services
High Street
Wombourne
Nr Wolverhampton WV5 9DN

Individual members of the British Mountaineering Council (BMC), or members of a Club affiliated to the BMC, can take advantage of specialist insurance by writing to:-

British Mountaineering Council
177-179 Burton Road
Manchester M20 2BB

Membership of the Austrian Alpine Club (UK Branch) automatically includes insurance for accident, mountain rescue and repatriation worldwide. For details write to:-

Austrian Alpine Club
P.O. Box 43

Welwyn Garden City AL8 6PQ

Finally, reciprocal medical arrangements in France are available for citizens of an EC country, details to be found in two DSS leaflets: *Medical Cover Abroad* and *Protect Your Health Abroad*. Obtain a copy of Form E111 from your local Post Office or DSS office, make a photocopy and take both copies with you when travelling abroad.

USING THE GUIDE

Throughout this guidebook metres and kilometres and standard feet and mile measurements have both been used. Metric measurements are taken directly from the map, where quoted, and then converted to the nearest British equivalent. In attempting to calculate the actual distance covered on each stage, I have made the best possible estimate, using the map as my guide. But with countless zigzags it's impossible to guarantee accuracy. At the head of the introduction to each stage I have quoted the amount of height gain and loss for that stage. Figures quoted are rough accumulations that should give walkers some idea of the strenuous nature (or otherwise) of the day ahead.

Times given for each stage, and part-stage, are likewise approximations only, but are quoted to give a rough indication of how long any particular section could take. They do *not* make allowances for rest stops, lunch breaks or photographic delays - so remember to add these to your estimate. No doubt times quoted here will be found slow by some walkers, fast by others. (Experience shows that the guidebook writer receives more complaints in respect of timing than any other reason!) All those given in this book were achieved by a reasonably fit, middle-aged walker carrying a sack that was too heavy, for long periods in dubious snow conditions. I've tried to be consistent, but variations are bound to occur. By comparing your own times with those quoted here (and on signposts along the way - which can sometimes be even more eccentric than my own) you should soon discover how much our pace differs and be able to calculate your own progress accordingly. I repeat, times are offered for rough guidance only. They are not provided as a challenge.

Where boxed paragraphs occur within the descriptive text, these relate to alternative trails, refuges accessible by a diversion from the standard tour, or make mention of a place of interest within walking distance. They have been isolated in boxes to avoid confusion with the main route described.

In the main body of text which follows, route directions 'left' and 'right' apply to the direction of travel, be that in ascent, descent or on a traverse. However, when used with reference to the banks of streams or glaciers, 'left' and 'right' indicate the direction of flow, ie. looking downwards. Where doubts might occur a compass direction is also provided.

Abbreviations appearing in the following pages are listed below:

BMC	-	British Mountaineering Council
CAF	-	Club Alpin Français
D&R	-	Didier & Richard (maps)
GR	-	Grande Randonnée
IGN	-	Institut Géographique National (maps)
PNV	-	Parc National de la Vanoise
PTT	-	Post Office (Post, Telephone & Telegraph)
Ref.	-	Refuge
TGV	-	Trains à Grande Vitesse
ToV	-	Tour of the Vanoise

*   *   *

Finally, routes described in this guide reflect as accurately as possible the Tour of the Vanoise as experienced during research. However, the mountain environment is not a static one, and changes can and do occur from time to time, resulting in paths being re-routed and certain landmarks altered. Any corrections required in order to keep the book up to date will be made in future printings where possible. Should you discover any changes that are necessary, or can recommend additions with regard to accommodation, I would appreciate a brief note to that effect. A postcard sent to me via the publisher would be gratefully received.

*   *   *

ROUTE PROFILE KEY

⌂	mountain refuge/hut
⌂	gîte d'étape
H	hotel
△	camping
▽	refreshments
	bus service
🚋	railway station
🚠	cable-car or chairlift
2hrs 15min	walking time from start of stage

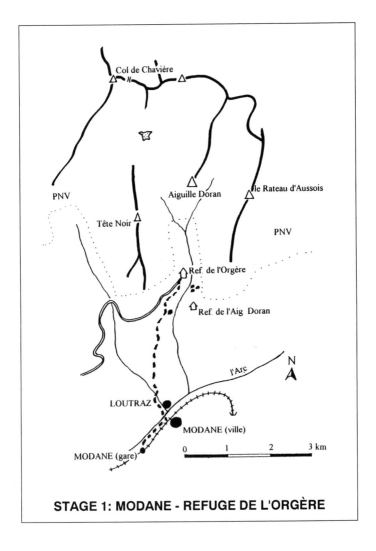

STAGE 1: MODANE - REFUGE DE L'ORGÈRE

The Route

STAGE 1:
MODANE - REFUGE DE L'ORGÈRE

Distance:	5.5 kilometres ($3^{1}/_{2}$ miles)
Time:	$2^{1}/_{2}$-3 hours
Start altitude:	1058m (3471ft)
High point:	Refuge de l'Orgère 1935m (6348ft)
Height gain:	877m (2877ft)
Accommodation:	Modane - hotels + camping
	Refuge de l'Aiguille Doran ($2^{1}/_{2}$hrs) - + camping
	Refuge de l'Orgère

This initial stage is necessarily short in the assumption that you arrive in Modane after a long journey from Britain, are eager to set out for the hills straight away, but are unable (or unwilling) to face a very full alternative doubling-up of stages to Plan Sec. In any case, the forest trail to Orgère is steep in places and will be sufficiently demanding to satisfy most walkers' ambitions for a start. It's a very pleasant stage, with light, spacious forest granting enough shade on a hot summer's day, and occasional open meadows bright with flowers. For much of the way views are gained of Modane in the valley below, and of the Charmaix glen cutting behind it into the Mont Thabor massif.

Coming from Chambéry, Modane has a rather depressed air about it. A small industrial town close to the Italian border (a road cuts above to the south and passes through the Tunnel de Fréjus into Italy, while the Chambéry-Turin railway also tunnels through the mountains here), its strategic position made it an important defensive stronghold, and perched on a bluff to the west it is protected by the sturdy-looking Fort du Sapey. This fortification was insufficient deterrent, however, to prevent Modane from being badly damaged during the second world war. Should you be in need of refreshment or accommodation, a choice of cafés, restaurants and hotels

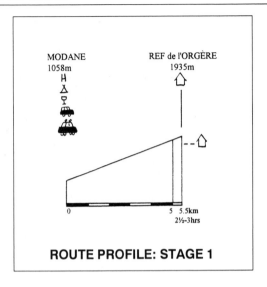

ROUTE PROFILE: STAGE 1

will be found near the station. A large supermarket edges the main road a short walk upvalley in the main part of town.

*　　*　　*

MODANE (1058m: 3471ft) *Hotels, camping, restaurants, shops, banks, PTT, railway link with Chambéry in about 1 hour, bus service for villages upvalley. Tourist information: Office de Tourisme, 73500 Modane (04 79 05 22 35). Hotels: du Commerce (04 79 05 00 78); de France (04 79 05 23 46); des Voyageurs (04 70 05 01 39); le Perce-Neige (04 79 05 00 50).*

On leaving the railway station bear right and wander along the main road heading upvalley. On coming to a road bridge over the River Arc you have a choice of routes. One option is to cross the bridge and follow a minor road which curves to the right and soon enters the suburb of Loutraz (occasional waymarks). The alternative remains on the south side of the river and allows an opportunity to stock up with last-minute provisions at the supermarket at Modane *ville* (the last opportunity for four days). The two routes rejoin in Loutraz.

The town square of Modane ville

Assuming the latter option is taken leave the main road just beyond the supermarket and turn left on a narrow road (signposted to le Bourget) which goes beneath the railway, then over the river to enter Loutraz. At a staggered crossroads go straight ahead rising uphill between houses - with red-white waymarks to guide you through the village. At another crossroads by a small chapel bear right. The road soon becomes a tree-lined track; when it forks bear right over a bridge. Winding uphill among trees the track narrows to a path.

Throughout the ensuing forest section, which leads almost all the way to l'Orgère, there are numerous trail junctions. Each one is signposted, or the route is otherwise obvious. Follow signs for Orgère. The path is clear and well-made, if narrow in places, and the forest a delight. As you gain height an alternative waymarked route eases away from that marked for Orgère, and is signposted to la Perrière - this is the GR55 route adopted also by GR5 in the past, although the direct route appears now to have superceded the la Perrière alternative. The direct route is steeper than the original, but avoids an unnecessarily devious road-walk.

Refuge de l'Orgère, a well-appointed hut built by the PNV

Eventually the Orgère trail emerges from forest into a lovely open meadow by the solitary stone chalet of **PIERRE BRUNE** (2¹/₂hrs), from which you gain impressive views eastward through the Haute-Maurienne. Across the meadow come onto a track where a sign gives 25 minutes to Refuge de l'Orgère.

Note: A 5 minute diversion along the track to the right leads to the privately-owned **REFUGE DE L'AIGUILLE DORAN** (1860m: 6102ft) *40 places, camping, meals provided, showers; open 15 May-15 Oct (04 72 12 58 70). Bookings when closed to: M Joël Portaz, 101 Rue des Quatre Vents, Villarodin - Le Bourget, 73500 Modane (04 79 20 34 51).*

Bear right for a few paces, then leave the track for a trail which rises above it on the left. The path re-enters forest, but makes an easy contour round the hillside and forks just below a minor road. The GR5 proper is the right-hand option, but we continue up to the road and a few paces along it come to a large building on the right-hand side.

REFUGE DE L'ORGÈRE (1935m: 6348ft) *Owned by the PNV, 56* *places, meals provided, kitchen facilities, showers; guardian 15 June-15 Sept (04 79 05 11 65). Winter room permanently open.*

*　　　*　　　*

This large and comfortable refuge (*a porte du parc,* or 'gateway to the park') overlooks pastures at the entrance to the Orgère glen, and enjoys views across to the south side of the Maurienne. As it stands at the entrance to the National Park and is accessible by road from Freney, downvalley of Modane, it is likely to be extra busy. During the summer months video films devoted to the wildlife of the region are often shown at the hut in the evenings as part of the National Park's education programme.

The sharp-pointed, pear-shaped Aiguille Doran (3041m: 9977ft) dominates the short Orgère glen north of the refuge. A nature trail (*sentier natur*) traverses the eastern flank of the valley, then curves at its head to join a track leading back to the hut, thus providing a pleasant circular walk. A high trail climbing directly above the refuge heads for Col de Chavière and Pralognan-la-Vanoise (see Stage 11 for a description of this in the reverse direction), while another which cuts along the eastern side of Aiguille Doran crosses Col de la Masse for an energetic and challenging route to Plan Sec. Our route to Plan Sec on Stage 2 is not quite as demanding, but is visually rewarding. The Orgère glen is rich in wild flowers in the early summer, and near its head chamois, marmots and bouquetin may be seen. Just below the refuge, on the route of GR5, stands an old and tiny chapel.

*　　　*　　　*

STAGE 2:
REFUGE DE L'ORGÈRE - COL DU BARBIER - REFUGE DU
PLAN SEC

Distance:	11 kilometres (7 miles)
Time:	4^{1}/$_2$ hours
Start altitude:	1935m (6348ft)
High point:	c.2400m (7874ft)
Height gain:	574m (1883ft)
Height loss:	181m (594ft)
Accommodation:	Refuge de l'Aiguille Doran (15mins) - + camping
	Refuge du Fond d'Aussois (3hrs + 30mins) - + camping
	Refuge de la Dent Parrachée (3^{1}/$_2$hrs + 30mins) - + camping
	Refuge du Plan Sec

This first full-day's stage provides plenty of scenic variety and serves as an excellent introduction to the area. The route to l'Orgère on Stage 1 gave little more than a hint, but the walk to Plan Sec gradually unfolds the topography of this southern edge of the Vanoise region. The trail mimics the National Park boundary for much of the way, follows a balcony along slopes high above the Maurienne, leads through forest and over steeply sloping pastures, soaks in a panorama of big mountains walling the south and east sides of the valley, and makes a great curve round a deeply-cut glen which contains a pair of small dammed lakes.

The first time we walked this route thick mist hid views for most of the way, only teasing now and then with a partial glimpse of rock peak and snowfield. Yet through the mists we spied chamois and bouquetin and sensed the grandeur of unseen landscapes. Next time we tackled it all was clear, and the full majestic variety was revealed. And along the path to the Barbier chalets we watched four baby marmots at play, close enough to touch.

Although the actual walking time needed for this stage is modest, in truth it will take much longer to get to your destination, for there's so much

Cascades wash cliffs that wall the route to Refuge de l'Arpont

La Grande Casse reflected in the mirror-like waters of Plan du Lac
The River Arc, near Bessans

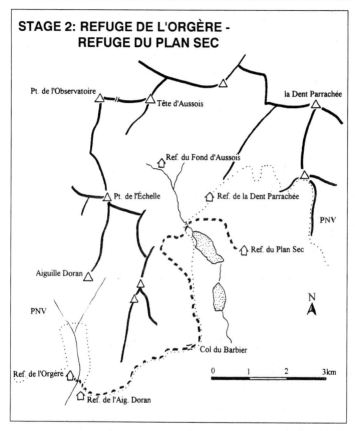

to see and enjoy along the way. It's not practicable to continue beyond Plan Sec, for the next hut is another 5¹/₂-6 hours further on. Plan Sec, however, is not the only option, for there's a choice of three huts in all. Both Fond d'Aussois and la Dent Parrachée are owned by the CAF, while Plan Sec is privately owned. Refuge du Fond d'Aussois is located in the upper levels of the glen, reached by a 30 minute diversion, while la Dent Parrachée is perched on a shelf nearly 200 metres (656ft) above the trail. Our route passes immediately below Plan Sec, which gives this refuge the edge over the other two.

33

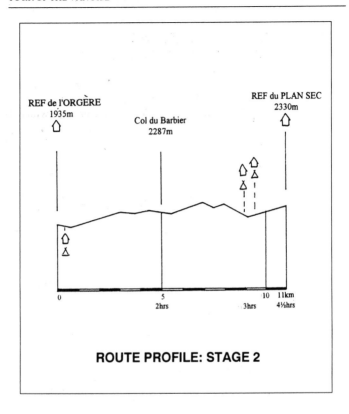

REF de l'ORGÈRE
1935m

Col du Barbier
2287m

REF du PLAN SEC
2330m

0   5   10   11km
          2hrs   3hrs 4½hrs

ROUTE PROFILE: STAGE 2

On leaving Refuge de l'Orgère two options present themselves. The most straightforward is to take a narrow path which descends directly from the hut and cuts through the pastures below, crosses a stream and comes onto a track. The alternative entails returning along the road to the forest edge to rejoin the GR5, along which you bear left and descend to a tiny chapel and a stone hut or two. This path is then joined by the direct trail mentioned above, crosses the stream and bears right along a track. Easy walking along the track brings you to a group of buildings, **L'ORGÈRE** (10mins) and a trail junction. Turn left, now entering forest.

Note: 300 metres (330yds) down the alternative path stands the **REFUGE DE L'AIGUILLE DORAN** (1860m: 6102ft) *Privately-owned, 40 places, camping, meals provided, showers; open 15 May-15 Oct (04 72 12 58 70). Bookings when closed to: M Joël Portaz, 101 Rue des Quatre Vents, Villarodin - Le Bourget, 73500 Modane (04 79 20 34 51).* A linking trail leads from the refuge back to the main Col du Barbier path, which it rejoins in forest.

At first, wandering through the forest, the trail follows a regular contour. Then it rises a little before losing height to the junction with the trail from Refuge de l'Aiguille Doran. Bear left at the junction. The way now begins to climb, crosses a small boulder tip followed by two minor streams, then steepens before coming to a high point of 2225 metres (7300ft) out of the trees. Here the path eases across high sloping pastures, rising slightly now and then, with fine views across and along the Maurienne where sentry-like peaks guard the valley.

Contouring a thousand metres (3280ft) or more above the valley bed the trail leads past a pair of stone buildings, **LE BARBIER** (1hr 50mins), and continues to wind along the indents of hillside, passes a ruin then descends to the broad grassy saddle of **COL DU BARBIER** (2287m: 7503ft 2hrs) from which the village of Aussois can be seen down in the valley.

The trail continues to descend and comes to another junction. Ignore the right-hand option which drops steeply to the dam at the southern end of the Plan d'Aval lake and continues to the valley. Instead take the left-hand trail heading northward along the west flank of a fine glen, on the far side of which Pointe de Bellecôte (3139m: 10,299ft) and La Dent Parrachée (3697m: 12,129ft) soar above the two gleaming lakes. A broad track may be seen carving a way across the lower slopes of these mountains, with a group of three tiny-looking buildings just above it: Refuge du Plan Sec.

In early summer this section of trail passes through a splash of crimson alpenroses. Views are enticing; not just the rim of mountains walling the glen, but the two lakes below; the first (Plan d'Aval) is the smaller and has a powerful cascade crashing into it from a 17 kilometre ($10^{1}/_{2}$ mile) pipe that diverts water through the mountains from the head of the Doron gorge, to serve the hydro station at

Avrieux; the upper lake (Plan d'Amont) is a deep green in colour and is the more attractive.

Climbing to a high point (2387m: 7831ft) the way then enters a broad, open area littered with rocks and running with streams. Crossing this, heading roughly north-west, the trail slopes gently downhill. Another path cuts off to the right. Ours continues into a gully to the left of a large rock-and grass-covered bluff, and rises through it hugging low crags in places. Another trail junction is met. (The left-hand branch here climbs to Col de la Masse (2923m: 9590ft) for a challenging route to Refuge de l'Orgère.) Bear right, crossing a stream (one or two cairns guide the way) to pass round the northern side of the bluff before descending steeply to a saddle of grass and alpenroses overlooking Plan d'Amont. The trail continues the descent to a track and a bridge over the torrent issuing from pastures in the upper reaches of the glen. This is **PONT DE LA SÉTÉRIA** (2206m: 7238ft 3hrs).

Note i: A 30 minute diversion left leads to **REFUGE DU FOND D'AUSSOIS** (2324m: 7625ft) *CAF-owned, 40 places, camping, meals provided, kitchen facilities, guardian July & August (04 79 20 39 83). Winter room permanently open.*

Note ii: The Aussois glen is linked with the valley of the Doron de Chavière to the north by Col d'Aussois (2916m: 9567ft). This col is crossed by walkers tackling the shorter *Tour des Glaciers de la Vanoise* on a strenuous route from Pralognan.

Cross the bridge and climb the slope ahead, taking care if late-winter snow still covers the trail on the initial steeply sloping section, then pass two more marked trail junctions. One offers the option of climbing left to reach yet another hut in 30 minutes.

REFUGE DE LA DENT PARRACHÉE (2511m: 8238ft) *CAF-owned, 29 places, camping, meals provided, kitchen facilities, guardian July & August (04 79 20 32 87). Winter room permanently open.* This hut is patronised by climbers tackling the ordinary route on La Dent Parrachée, upon whose lower south-west ridge (Arêtes de l'Eche) it is ideally situated.

Below a stone building, **LA FOURNACHE** (2330m: 7644ft), cut down across pastures and over two streams draining the Vallon de la Fournache. A few paces beyond the second of these bear left up a path which rises directly to a dirt road/track. Turn right along this for about 15 minutes when the three buildings of Plan Sec will be seen just above it. A signposted path leads directly to them.

REFUGE DU PLAN SEC (c2330m: 7644ft) *Privately-owned, 80 places, meals provided, kitchen facilities, showers; open mid-June to mid-September (04 79 20 31 31).*

*   *   *

Plan Sec has been converted from a summer farm, the three low stone buildings squat among the pastures gazing west across the glen to a rugged outline of peaks. One of the buildings is given over to dormitory accommodation. One is split-level and contains the guardian's living quarters with the communal dining room (which used to be the stable) below. The third houses toilets, showers and self-catering kitchen. Downvalley a short distance away a few ski-lifts lace the hillside. Plan Sec and the dammed lakes below it lie just outside the National Park boundary.

*   *   *

STAGE 3:
REFUGE DU PLAN SEC - REFUGE DE L'ARPONT

Distance:	18 kilometres (11 miles)
Time:	5¹/₂-6 hours
Start altitude:	2330m (7644ft)
High point:	2438m (7999ft)
Height gain:	486m (1594ft)
Height loss:	338m (1109ft)
Accommodation:	Refuge de l'Arpont - + camping

On the way from Plan Sec to l'Arpont the Tour of the Vanoise begins to experience the true nature of this remarkable region. Rounding the southern spur of Pointe de Bellecôte the trail gains a hint of a more wild and robust

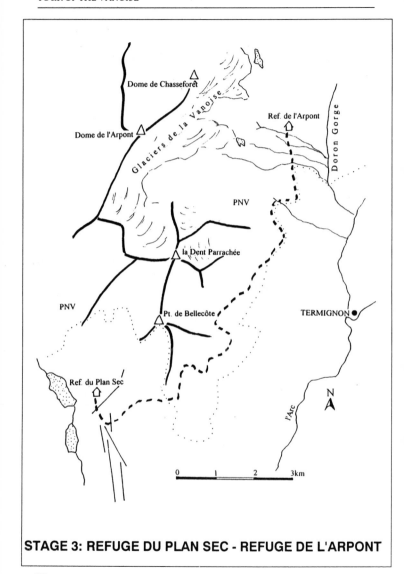

STAGE 3: REFUGE DU PLAN SEC - REFUGE DE L'ARPONT

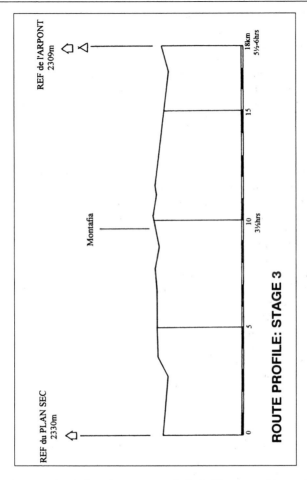

ROUTE PROFILE: STAGE 3

country; a contrast of rough upper crags dashed with snow and ice, and soft low-lying pasture with forest at mid-height. Then, curving round indented combes and rough little glens, and climbing over more projecting spurs, suddenly the deep gash of the Doron gorge is seen slicing through the mountains; mountains that grow in stature towards the north - that will be seen in all their glory on Stage 4.

As you draw near to l'Arpont, so the hanging glaciers of Belle Place, Mahure and Dôme de l'Arpont send down their melt in cascades that spray over shining cliffs, and the final approach crosses one glacial stream after another that are systematically carving mini-gorges through the tilted plateau overlooked by the hut. Bouquetin frequent the meadows and rocky places that form a terrace above the gorge, and are often seen grazing near the hut, while marmots may be seen almost anywhere on this stage of the walk.

*　　*　　*

Departing Plan Sec descend to the track and bear left along it. Just before reaching the ski tows the track forks. Take the lower option which continues straight ahead, and when it makes a right-hand hairpin soon after, leave the track for a footpath going off slightly left ahead through pastures, with views across to the south side of the Maurienne valley.

The route now makes a steady traverse of grass slopes high above the valley, working roughly north-east. The slope steepens, though the trail contours, and a short section is safeguarded by a fixed chain where the path is interrupted by a brief cut (the IGN map marks this as difficult, but it's hardly that). Beyond this come to a gully, bear left into it and climb by way of zigzags to a trail junction. One path continues to climb to Grasse Combe. Our route swings right and edges against the base of cliffs before making a rising traverse that climbs after a while in lazy windings to gain a broad grass saddle and another trail junction, **LA TURRA** (2326m: 7631ft 1hr).

Note: The right-hand trail here descends to the village of Sardières by way of the *Monolithe de Sardières*, a 93 metre (305ft) tooth of rock jutting from the forest, that attracts tourists and climbers alike.

Take the wide path breaking off slightly left ahead. This makes a generous winding ascent of the slopes of Roc de Corneilles before easing right on a long contouring traverse of a steep-walled combe, at the far side of which you reach a second grass saddle and yet another junction of paths. Ruins may be seen below the trail on the right. This is **LA LOZA** (2360m: 7743ft 2hrs 15mins). If you stray for a moment to the small hill east of the junction, extensive views are to be had which include La Grande Casse and La Grande Motte some way to the north beyond the Doron gorge.

Once again the contouring trail veers slightly left from this saddle (the right-hand path descends to Sardières), and enters another combe below Pointe de Bellecôte drained by the Bonne Nuit stream. The trail is clear, though narrow in places, and early in the season may be wearing snowfields - in which case take care when crossing these. At one point the trail picks a way across a rockfall. Far below, Termignon can be seen at the confluence of two valleys - that of the Arc (Haute-Maurienne), which breaks off to the east, and of the Doron flowing from the north.

Across the combe the path climbs to a high point (2438m: 7999ft), then descends to cross a smaller combe with streams running through it. Over the main stream the trail starts to rise once more and tops a bluff (**MONTAFIA** 3$^{1/2}$hrs) with a ruined building at a trail junction. (The right-hand option makes a steep descent to Termignon in 1$^{1/2}$ hours.) Our path continues to rise, steadily at first, then more steeply in zigzags, before cutting into a shallow glen, Combe d'Enfer, at the head of which hangs the Glacier de la Mahure which, together with other icefields making an apron below the Dômes du Génépy, forms the southern limit of the Glaciers de la Vanoise - the major icesheet of the whole Vanoise region.

Combe d'Enfer is a delight of streams, cascades, crags, rough pastures and alpenroses. Descending eastwards on the north bank of the glen the way passes a simple-looking alp farm advertising cheese, drinks and basic accommodation (*couchettes*). A few minutes later come to a group of buildings and ruins, **LE MONT** (4$^{1/2}$hrs). Another path descends from here to Termignon, while ours continues ahead, now high above the Doron gorge, sneaking through alder thickets. As the way progresses so the vegetation changes and alpenroses grow in bright patches along the hillside. The slab face of the Pointe de la Réchasse appears to be blocking the head of the valley, and entices from the north. Other big mountains crowd the horizon, and soon the Refuge de l'Arpont may be spied upon its hillside perch ahead.

The valley grows more beautiful and inspiring the deeper you wander through. Waterfalls cascade from cliffs on the left. One footbridge after another takes the trail across streams digging channels

Refuge de l'Arpont

through the rock; there are a few ruined stone hutments on either side of the path, the Chapelle St-Laurent standing beside the trail, and a little farm; then more streams to cross, green pastures starred with flowers and hanging glaciers high above to the left. Then the trail makes its final slant up an easy slope to gain the hut.

REFUGE DE L'ARPONT (2309m: 7575ft) *Owned by the PNV, 95 places, camping, meals provided, kitchen facilities, showers; guardian from end May-mid Sept (04 79 20 51 51). Winter room permanently open.*

*   *   *

Built in the early '70s, the hut has a magnificent outlook. Although mountains at the head of the valley cannot be seen from it (you have to walk up the trail a short distance to gain these views), it commands all the valley to the south from its prominent position on the south flank of a spur jutting from Dôme de Chasseforêt. The Doron gorge is a shadowed hint below, the gleam of snow and ice forms a pelmet above to the west. Bouquetin can often be seen grazing nearby.

West of the hut the Glacier de l'Arpont is draped down the face of Dôme de l'Arpont, a frozen cascade of séracs and crevasses; a fine sight, albeit barely visible from the refuge. At the foot of the glacier, some 357 metres (1171ft) above the hut, lies a small tarn, Lac de l'Arpont. Given time, energy and favourable conditions, it would be worth scrambling up to this tarn to enjoy its prestigious situation and some tremendous views. The trail which heads west from the hut is the one to take. After climbing fairly steeply for a while it fades away, but is replaced by a vague line of cairns. The route is rough and strenuous, the terrain rocky, but the effort will be repaid. Allow $2^{1}/2$ hours for the round trip.

*   *   *

STAGE 4:
REFUGE DE L'ARPONT - REFUGE DU PLAN DU LAC

Distance:	12 kilometres ($7^{1}/2$ miles)
Time:	5 hours
Start altitude:	2309m (7575ft)
High point:	c2580m (8465ft)
Low point:	2011m (6598ft)
Height gain:	624m (2047ft)
Height loss:	569m (1867ft)
Accommodation:	Refuge d'Entre Deux Eaux (3hrs 15mins + 10mins)
	Refuge de la Femma (3hrs 15mins + 2hrs)
	Refuge du Plan du Lac

This particular stage is one of the great walks of the tour; a horseshoe loop with tremendous views practically every step of the way, a varied terrain, a good possibility of watching wildlife, a bounty of alpine flowers, and prospects of diverting into another valley for those so inclined. The basic route hiccups its way along the western hillside heading north under the Glaciers de la Vanoise towards Mont Pelve, Pointe de la Réchasse, Pointe Mathews (the south summit of La Grande Casse), and with the big wall linking that King of the Vanoise with La Grande Motte forming a major feature at the head of the Doron valley. A number of streams are crossed, a huge moraine bank and various icy tarns skirted, and pastures wandered before descending steeply to the confluence of the Leisse and Rocheure

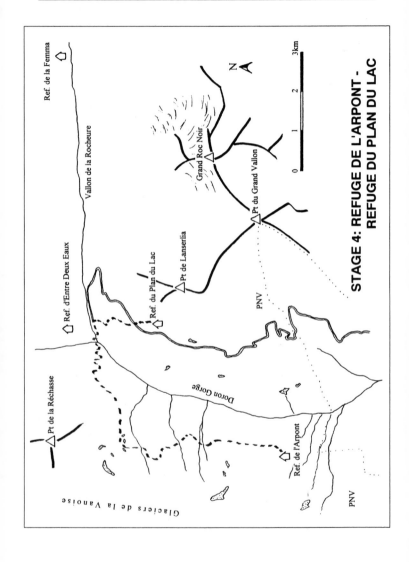

STAGE 4: REFUGE DE L'ARPONT -
REFUGE DU PLAN DU LAC

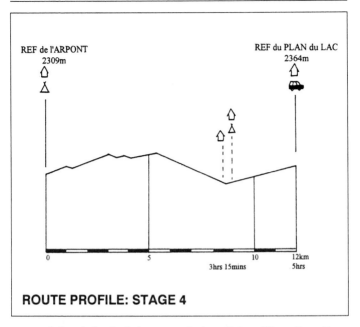

ROUTE PROFILE: STAGE 4

torrents below the lovely alp farm turned private Refuge d'Entre Deux Eaux. The way now curves southward across the mouth of the Vallon de la Rocheure, climbs a grass- and shrub-covered hillside and reaches the PNV-owned Refuge du Plan du Lac, with its charming views west to the dazzling snow and ice of the Glaciers de la Vanoise.

Walkers tackling only the western circuit, the Tour des Glaciers de la Vanoise, will leave the main route on this stage by adopting a high trail which breaks away from the path descending to the pastures below Entre Deux Eaux, and traverse instead the eastern slopes of Pointe de la Réchasse before joining the standard route to Col de la Vanoise and Pralognan. An outline of this circuit is given elsewhere in this guide, following the main tour description.

An alternative option would be to follow the main route as described as far as the mouth of the Vallon de la Rocheure, but instead of climbing south to Plan du Lac, continue eastward through the Rocheure glen to spend a night at Refuge de la Femma. Sufficient time would then be available next day to explore this beautiful glen before returning downvalley, and then walking up to Refuge du Plan du Lac, thus adding a day to the overall tour. A visit to the Rocheure glen (via Entre Deux Eaux) is, in fact, suggested as an optional extra later in the tour after leaving Refuge de la Leisse. For details, see Alternative Stage 9.

*   *   *

Heading upvalley from l'Arpont the trail strikes north-eastward from the hut, then rises to the north, soon with grand views to a group of big mountains blocking the valley in an impressive amphitheatre. Care is required when snow remains on this section of the path, which is exposed in places. Reaching a high shelf the way then descends a little to cross a shallow basin, beyond which you rise to a minor plateau - a gently sloping hillside dotted with small pools and with streams sidling through, ready to tip into the gorge of the Doron de la Rocheure (also known as the Doron de Termignon). The trail skirts the left-hand side of this plateau while the cliffs of Mont Pelve (3261m: 10,699ft), Roche Ferran (3099m: 10,167ft) and Pointe de la Réchasse (3212m: 10,538ft) soar out of the landscape ahead in a formidable wall. Refuge du Plan du Lac may be seen to the east across the head of the Doron gorge.

Cross a grassy bluff, then descend leftwards into a basin below the Glacier du Pelve whose moraine bank towers on the north side.

Note: Above this moraine to the north, walled by the upper crags of Roche Ferran, will be found the beautiful Lac de la Roche Ferran and the smaller Lac du Pelve; a classic site. It's possible to gain these tarns by following up the bank of the Letta stream.

A glacial torrent is crossed on a footbridge, then the trail veers right to follow along the stream's left bank before curving to cross a second torrent. After this the route passes between a pair of small tarns, the Lacs de Lozières, goes up some glacier-polished slabs, passes above another tarn and continues to climb gently with fine views ahead. At one point it is possible to see down into the head of the Doron gorge, while the Vallon de la Rocheure stretches enticingly ahead in the east. Above the entrance to that glen an impressive

Walkers breaking trail through the snow above the Lacs de Lozières

shattered crest towers over green pastures. Looking back the Glaciers de la Vanoise show as a vast dome of ice and snow.

Set upon a high rolling grassland, not far from where the path begins to descend to the confluence of two valleys, a large 'acorn cup' stone is thought to have been carved by Neolithic man. A short way down this descent path come to a signpost and a trail junction (2329m: 7641ft 2hrs 45mins).

Note: The left-hand option makes a traverse of the rocky eastern wall of Pointe de la Réchasse, then skirts left through a shallow glen to gain Col de la Vanoise in about two hours. The trail is mostly clear and straightforward, crossing screes and boulderslopes in its initial balcony stage, before joining the GR55 at a trail junction near a large triangular memorial stone. From this junction to Col de la Vanoise the route is described under Stage 9. **REFUGE DU COL DE LA VANOISE** (2517m: 8258ft) *CAF-owned, 154 places, meals provided, kitchen facilities, guardian mid June to mid Sept (04 79 22 96 60). Winter room permanently open.*

Our route continues down, a steep trail twisting in numerous zigzags until joining a farm track just below a stone-built barn near the chalets of La Para. The gradient eases, but you desert the track again in favour of a narrow path by a ruin, and cut down through pastures to the valley bed. Follow a track round to the Doron river and wander alongside it upstream to the confluence of two streams; the first is Torrent de la Leisse, the second the Torrent de la Rocheure. Cross a bridge over the first and continue on the track to cross the second.

Note: To visit **REFUGE D'ENTRE DEUX EAUX** (2120m: 6955ft) *Privately-owned, 60 places, meals provided, kitchen facilities, showers, open summer only (04 79 20 50 85)* do not cross the second bridge but follow a signposted trail uphill to the left, reaching the hut in about 10 minutes.

Over the second bridge wander up a tarmac road for about 300 metres (330yds), then break away to the right on a footpath signposted to Porte du Parc.

Alternative Route: The alternative option mentioned in the introduction to this Stage, which entails wandering through the Rocheure glen to the la Femma hut, leaves the main route at this point. Follow the road heading east for about 1.5 kilometres (1 mile) until it makes a sharp hairpin to the right. Now continue ahead on a track that works its way deeper into the Vallon de la Rocheure, crosses to the north bank of the river, and soon after ends at the Chalet de la Rocheure. A footpath continues over pastures and in 30 minutes (2 hours from the start of this diversion) comes to **REFUGE DE LA FEMMA** (2323m: 7621ft) *PNV-owned, 48 places, camping, meals provided, kitchen facilities, showers, guardian in summer (04 79 20 50 85). Winter room permanently open.*

The continuing main route to Plan du Lac climbs easily among lush vegetation, passes below a cascade, and steadily gains height to reach a large rolling grassland. Come onto the road again by the Chapelle St-Barthélémy, bear right for a few paces, then left to rise

---

Frontier peaks, adorned with glaciers, focus the trekker's attention from a balcony viewpoint in the Lenta gorge

Bonneval-sur-Arc, seen from the steeply climbing trail at the start of Stage 7
On the proverbial clear day Mont Blanc can be seen from Pas de la Tovière

through open pastures to a col with an orientation table. Just beyond this you will reach the hut, although 'hut' is hardly the word with which to describe this neat, stone-built refuge with its parasol-shaded tables outside and waitress service.

REFUGE DU PLAN DU LAC (2364m: 7756ft) *Owned by the PNV, 60 places, meals provided, kitchen facilities, showers, guardian mid June to end of Sept (04 79 20 50 85). Winter room permanently open.*

*　　*　　*

This is a popular, well-appointed hut made extra-busy by virtue of the road which passes nearby. No private vehicles are permitted along this road beyond Bellecombe, a parking area less than an hour's walk to the south, but a summer shuttle bus service (*navette*) ferries passengers between Termignon, in the Maurienne, and the Pont de la Rocheure below Entre Deux Eaux. This *navette* is patronised by day-trippers in the high summer, as well as by walkers and climbers who use it to short-cut an otherwise long approach from the Haute-Maurienne.

Refuge du Plan du Lac enjoys a favoured location, set as it is on flat meadows with extensive views west across the unseen Doron gorge to the Glaciers de la Vanoise, and north to La Grande Casse (3855m: 12,648ft) and La Grande Motte (3653m: 11,985ft). The position of Col de la Vanoise, by which Pralognan is reached later on our tour (Stage 9), is hinted by a deep notch seen to the left of La Grande Casse. The highest summit in the Vanoise Alps, La Grande Casse received its first ascent in 1860 from William Mathews, one of the founders of the Alpine Club, and his guide Michel Croz, who was to die tragically following the first ascent of the Matterhorn in 1865. The great summit dome and glaciers of La Grande Motte, just visible above the stern wall of the Vallon de la Leisse, are laced with ski tows and cableways made accessible from Val Claret, which has resulted in an unnatural indent in the National Park's boundary line.

A short walk west of the hut provides a spectacular view into the Doron gorge, while the beautiful Plan du Lac lake is reached in 10 minutes heading downvalley. The eastern shoreline of this is skirted on Stage 5.

*　　*　　*

STAGE 5:
REFUGE DU PLAN DU LAC - REFUGE DU CUCHET - REFUGE DU VALLONBRUN

Distance:	18 kilometres (11 miles)
Time:	6 hours
Start altitude:	2364m (7756ft)
High point:	2473m (8114ft)
Low point:	1990m (6529ft)
Height gain:	448m (1470ft)
Height loss:	540m (1772ft)
Accommodation:	Refuge du Cuchet (4hrs)
	Refuge du Vallonbrun - + camping

The longest stage so far, but fortunately, perhaps, there are few steep uphill sections to counterbalance a rather wearisome descent from the ridge-spur of Crête de la Turra which effectively marks the south-eastern end of the Doron valley. The trail is a good one nearly all the way from Plan du Lac to Vallonbrun. A scenically interesting one, too, for the day begins with those classic views across the Doron gorge to the Glaciers de la Vanoise, soon adds high mountain reflections in the waters of Plan du Lac, exchanges these for a panorama that includes much of the route of the Tour de la Vanoise wandered two days ago, then south across the Haute-Maurienne to Col du Mont Cenis and Pointe de Ronce.

Before the route turns away from the Doron valley's influence, it curves round a vast open pastoral hillside below the Crête de Côte Chaude - almost amphitheatre-like in its formation. A few small farmsteads stand dwarfed by the enormity of this hillside and overlook the serpentine writhings of the road to Termignon, while La Dent Parrachée dominates the view west.

Once the Crête de la Turra has been turned the trail descends steeply into forest before a track progresses the route eastward. The former route of the GR5 passed below the unmanned Refuge du Cuchet (a short trail diverted to it), and later climbed very steeply past a few ruins to avoid a band of cliffs before heading east again on a high belvedere 700 metres (2297ft) or so above the valley. But a more direct path has now been made which is kinder to tired legs; it goes up to the Cuchet hut then continues past it on a linking trail, thus saving a nasty climb at the wrong end of the day

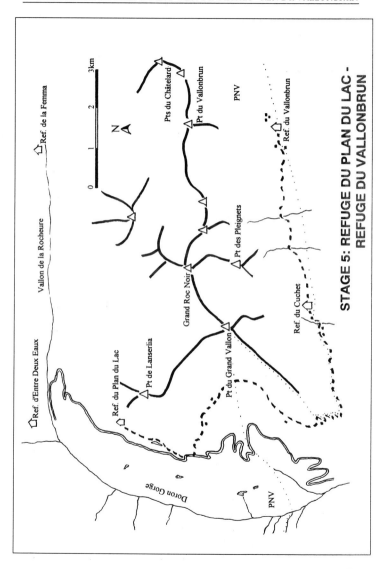

STAGE 5: REFUGE DU PLAN DU LAC - REFUGE DU VALLONBRUN

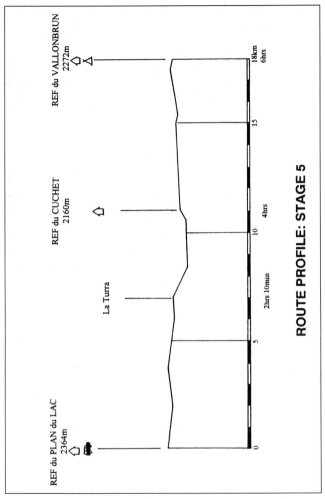

ROUTE PROFILE: STAGE 5

REF du PLAN du LAC 2364m

La Turra

REF du CUCHET 2160m

REF du VALLONBRUN 2272m

0   5   2hrs 10min   10   4hrs   15   18km 6hrs

Departing Plan du Lac head south on an easy path across almost level pastureland, and in about 10 minutes come to the lake at an altitude of 2400 metres (7874ft), which in clear conditions and looking north provides wonderful inverted views of La Grande Casse and La

52

Grande Motte. Pass along the left-hand (eastern) side of the lake and soon after cut through a grassy cleft in the hills. Once through this, peaks on the south side of the Maurienne valley show as a pleasant wall some way ahead. The trail descends to **BELLECOMBE** (2307m: 7569ft 30mins), a large parking area and bus stop for the shuttle service between Termignon and the Pont de la Rocheure. Wander down the road a short distance, and when it begins a right-hand curve, break away left on a track signposted to Refuge du Cuchet in 3hrs 15mins.

Almost immediately the track forks. Take the left-hand option. It winds comfortably round broad rolling pastures and soon shows the huge curving basin of hillside topped by the Crête de Côte Chaude through which the route progresses. Pass a small farm building on the right of the track (cheese, butter and eggs for sale) and continue as far as another farm, **LA FEMMA** (1¹/₂hrs) where the track ends. A narrow footpath leads on, sweeping round the hillside bay. It rises gently, then loses a little height and affords fine views back to the north towards the head of the valley of the Doron de la Rocheure, and over to the west where the trail to l'Arpont, taken on Stage 3, can be seen.

Pass another small group of farm buildings, and shortly after join a farm track. When it forks take the left-hand branch rising ahead. Just after being joined by another coming from the right, top a rise, veer left and cross a spur of the Crête de la Turra at **LA TURRA DE TERMIGNON** (2290m: 7513ft 2hrs 10mins) effectively forming the gateway to the Doron valley. This is an impressive site. Termignon is almost 1000 metres (3281ft) below, and at the edge of the crest two contrasting valleys, with different vegetation and different mountain architecture, are spread out for inspection.

The trail now descends steeply past the Chalets de la Turra de Termignon, goes through a natural rock garden, then enters forest. The way is unrelentingly steep and twisting, losing some 300 metres (984ft) of altitude before coming to a crossing track marked as **PRÉ VAILLANT** (1990m: 6529ft 2hrs 40mins) where you turn left, now cutting through the Bois de Fontaniou. When it emerges from the forest by a stone barn the track leads between open meadows and winds gently on, tracing a regular contour and with views along the Maurienne valley.

Just before coming to a stone-built chalet a footpath cuts off left, signposted to Refuge du Cuchet. Follow this path above the chalet, past a few ruins and on to a stream above the farm buildings of le Cuchet. Immediately over this the path forks. The left-hand option climbs to Refuge du Cuchet and then follows a high belvedere trail to Vallonbrun. The path ahead is the original GR5 which leads to Vallonbrun without visiting Refuge du Cuchet. It's a longer and more tiring route, but is offered below as an alternative option.

Bear left and climb steeply for about 15 minutes to reach **REFUGE DU CUCHET** (2160m: 7087ft 4hrs) *Owned by PNV, 24 places, kitchen facilities, unmanned, permanently open.* The hut is perched high above the valley on a small spur of hillside. There's a path junction just before it, the right-hand trail descending to join the alternative GR5 route. Ignore this and pass alongside the hut, then continue ahead on a high route that cuts along the steeply-plunging mountainside, crosses a couple of ravines, and is rejoined by the GR5 alternative at a stream.

Alternative GR5 Original Route: Over the stream ignore the path which climbs to Refuge du Cuchet and continue on a fairly even contour to the ruins of **PRAMARIA** where there's another trail junction. The left-hand path here also climbs to Refuge du Cuchet, while our route straight ahead is signposted to Lanslevillard. It's a thin trail that works its way across the hillside, loses then gains height, cuts into a tight ravine, and just beyond this comes to more ruins and yet another trail junction. This is **LE COIN BAS**, with one path descending to Lanslevillard (1hr), while ours turns left to climb a series of steep zigzags. The way then eases along a contour to the ruins of le Coin Haut. Just beyond these cross a stream and climb again to join the direct high route from Refuge du Cuchet at another stream. Bear right.

The high path crosses two more narrow ravines and continues easily along the hillside before curving into a large combe below the Grand Roc Noir (3582m: 11,752ft). Cross a major stream which drains through the combe, and go up a slope to a junction of paths at **PLA DE LA CHA** (2400m: 7874ft 5hrs 15mins).

Note: Another path cuts off left here and climbs to the curious *Pierre-aux-Pieds*, a huge block of schistose rock on which dozens of small feet were carved, possibly 7000 years ago.

Bear slightly right to climb a moraine bank, then veer left. At a crossing track bear right then left on the continuing path. One further hillside spur is crossed, then you descend on a gentle sloping path into the secretive little glen-like pastureland of Vallonbrun. Pass a few farm buildings of la Fesse du Milieu (note the overlapping slab roofs) and come onto a narrow road directly opposite the Vallonbrun hut.

REFUGE DU VALLONBRUN (2272m: 7454ft) *Owned by PNV, 45 places, camping, meals provided, kitchen facilities, guardian mid June to mid Sept (04 79 05 93 93). Winter room permanently open.*

*   *   *

This is a small, comfortable, split-level refuge with character all its own. The dining/common room/kitchen area is entered from the

Refuge du Vallonbrun

eastern side, while the dormitory and washroom are both set below and reached from the south. The designated camping area is found above the hut on a grassy bluff to the south.

Vallonbrun is a gentle, peaceful back-country, with good views south across the deep and narrow Haute-Maurienne to the Glacier de l'Arcelle Neuve draped across the face of Signal du Grand Mont Cenis, with Pointe de Ronce just to the east of that wearing its own icy shawl. The hut also provides good views west, too, while its eastern outlook is limited by the rise of the glen leading to a small chapel and a handful of chalets at the hamlet of la Fesse d'en haut.

High above the glen to the north a long wall of mountains, topped by the Grand Roc Noir, stretches eastward before curving gently to the north-east, unbroken between the Doron valley and the Col de l'Iseran and rarely dropping below 3000 metres (9842ft). Several glaciers lie tucked below that ridge wall, but most of these drain northward into the Rocheure glen.

*   *   *

STAGE 6:

REFUGE DU VALLONBRUN - BESSANS - BONNEVAL-SUR-ARC

Distance:	16 kilometres (10 miles)
Time:	4¹/₂ hours
Start altitude:	2272m (7454ft)
High point:	2300m (7546ft)
Low point:	1674m (5492ft)
Height loss:	626m (2054ft)
Height gain:	141m (463ft)
Accommodation:	Bessans (2hrs 10mins) - hotels + camping
	Refuge du Molard (2hrs 20mins + 1¹/₂hrs)
	le Villaron (2hrs 45mins) - gîte d'étape
	Bonneval - hotels, Chalet-Refuge du Bonneval

For the first time since setting out from Modane this stage revisits the Arc valley (known here as the Haute-Maurienne) and provides an opportunity

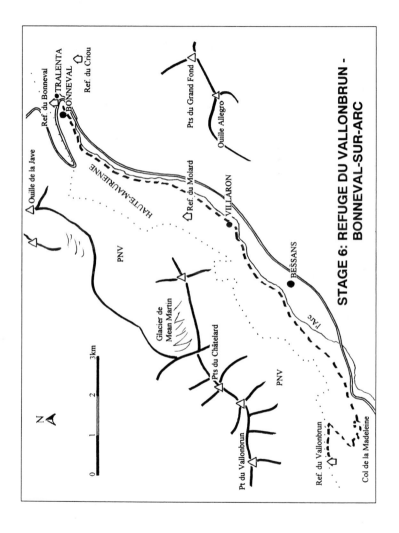

STAGE 6: REFUGE DU VALLONBRUN - BONNEVAL-SUR-ARC

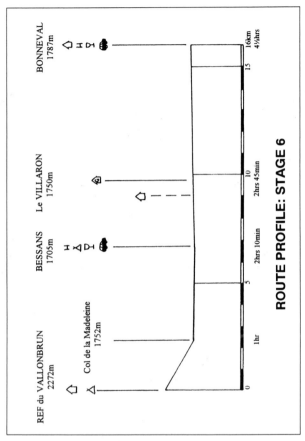

ROUTE PROFILE: STAGE 6

to restock with supplies. By temporarily deserting the high country the Tour of the Vanoise is not being disloyal - there's no alternative - but in fact rewards the trekker with a fresh perspective. The valley walk from Col de la Madeleine to Bonneval-sur-Arc has much to commend it; especially in the early summer when the meadows are in full bloom. A short detour gives access to Bessans; the trail passes through the hamlet of le Villaron, and the stage ends in the finest of all Maurienne villages, Bonneval, where vernacular architecture blends with a magical effect at the foot of the mountains.

Outside Bessans an alternative path returns to the high mountainside, passes Refuge du Molard and is later joined by the main trail in the Vallon de la Lenta glen on the way to Col de l'Iseran described under Stage 7. The problem with taking this alternative is that the only option for overnight accommodation (the Molard hut) really comes too early in the day. But continue beyond that and you'll either have to descend to Bonneval or double up to Val d'Isère, making a hefty 10-11 hour day, plus rests. The stage as described (the valley route is known as the 'Sentier du Petit Bonheur') gives a fairly easy buffer between two quite hard days.

*　　　*　　　*

The day begins by walking up the dirt road for about 200 metres to reach the little **CHAPELLE ST-ANTOINE** (2300m: 7546ft). Immediately beyond this take a footpath signposted to Col de la Madeleine which slopes directly ahead through pastures. At a junction of paths bear right and soon pass a collection of ruins. The trail steepens in zigzags, descending a hillside lavish with flowers, and eventually reaches the valley floor at **COL DE LA MADELEINE** (1752m: 5748ft 1hr) and the hamlet of Collet - several stone chalets and a small chapel built in 1603. A tremendous landslip once blocked the valley here, and the consequent build-up of water created a huge lake where now lies the Bessans plain.

Bear left along the road for a few paces, but when it begins to veer right by a ruin, take a narrow path breaking away to the left. This leads along a little raised 'causeway' between meadows (magnificent with flowers before the grass has been cut) and with lovely views ahead. The way is obvious, and it eventually leads onto the main valley road where you continue ahead for a short distance until it makes a right-hand curve. Leave the road for a track which cuts off left to **LA CHALP**. The track eases along the valley and after about an hour from the road brings you to a bridge leading across the Arc to Bessans.

BESSANS (1705m: 5594ft 2hrs 10mins) *Hotels, camping, restaurants, shops, PTT. Tourist information: Office de Tourisme, 73480 Bessans (04 70 05 96 52). Hotels: le Chamois (04 79 05 94 87); le Grand Fond (04 79 05 83 05); Mont Iseran (04 79 05 95 97); la Vanoise (04 79 05 96 79). The village* was largely destroyed by enemy action in 1944, but has been rebuilt in traditional style. Tradition remains very much a part of Bessans, not only in its architecture, for during major festivals local costume is still worn by the villagers. The Chapelle St-Antoine, dating from the 14th century, but restored 500 years later, contains a number of 15th century frescos, while murals depicting both virtues and vices adorn external walls.

The route does not cross to Bessans, but remains on the north bank of the river as a track, and about 10 minutes from the bridge comes to a junction.

Note: The left-hand option, an insignificant-looking path, is the alternative GR5 route via **REFUGE DU MOLARD** (2230m: 7316ft 1¹/₂hrs from here) *PNV-owned, 14 places, kitchen facilities, unmanned, permanently open.*

Continue along the track a little further. Soon take a footpath that strikes through a small woodland, then hugs pastures alongside the river before joining another track winding between more meadows. (On the opposite side of the valley the narrow Vallée d'Avérole cuts back deeply into the mountain wall north of Pointe de Charbonnel; a wild glen with three tiny villages, a refuge and some savage mountain scenery.) The meadow-lined track leads directly to **LE VILLARON** (1750m: 5741ft 2hrs 45mins) where there's accommodation to be had in a *gîte d'étape* close to the hamlet entrance. **GÎTE DU VILLARON** *33 places, meals provided, kitchen facilities, open Dec-Sept (04 79 05 95 84).*

Follow the road as it curves out of the hamlet (note the small chapel with a cross bearing symbols of the Passion), but then leave it for another track cutting ahead at a sharp right-hand bend. The track is signposted to Bonneval. Remaining on the true right bank (west side) of the river, it continues between meadows and through patches of woodland, curves beneath the huge black-streaked block of Rocher Chateau on which prehistoric paintings depicting deer have been discovered, then stops at a small stream. A footpath continues from it, passing through yet more fine meadows as the valley opens in a long and gentle curve to the north-east, and leads directly to Bonneval.

BONNEVAL-SUR-ARC (1787m: 5863ft) *Hotels, refuge, shops, restaurants, PTT. Tourist information: Office de Tourisme, 73480 Bonneval-sur-Arc (04 79 05 95 95). Chalet-Refuge du Bonneval, owned by CAF (04 79 05 95 07). Hotels: la Bergerie (04 79 05 94 97); du Glacier des Evettes (04 79 05 94 06); la Marmotte (04 79 05 94 82); à la Pastourelle (04 79 05 81 56).*

*   *   *

Most of the new development, including some of Bonneval's hotels, tourist information and National Park information offices, is located in the hamlet 'suburb' of Tralenta at the foot of the Col de l'Iseran road. Should all accommodation be taken, try the privately-owned **REFUGE DU CRIOU** *16 places, meals provided, guardian in summer, and from 15 Dec to end April (04 79 05 95 44).* (This refuge is situated on the hillside above and to the south-east of Tralenta. It has been known for the guardian to collect guests from the tourist information office, drive them to his hut by 4WD and return them to the start of the route next morning!)

Bonneval is a delight of well-kept medieval stone houses huddled one against another at the foot of the steeply sloping hillside on the west bank of the Arc. Varnished balconies hung with geraniums and petunias bring colour to the narrow streets; arched doorways and a jigsaw puzzle of stone slab roofs stained here and there with rust-coloured lichens provide a timeless quality - there are no external television aerials or electricity cables to suggest a modern world, and visitors' cars are banned from the centre of the village. But in some respects Bonneval is almost too perfect, and as it has been preserved very much as a showcase, it attracts hordes of tourists. It must be hard to live there, although a night spent in one of the village hotels makes a very pleasant interval on our tour.

Beyond Bonneval and Tralenta the recently-restored hamlet of L'Écot is the highest in the valley. Above it to the south-east tower glacier-adorned peaks that form the Italian frontier. Some good walking country exists on the slopes below the glaciers, with the CAF-owned Refuge des Evettes providing accommodation for walkers and climbers on the Plan des Evettes at 2616 metres (8583ft). A trail links the Evettes and Criou huts high above the valley along the north flank of Ouille Mouta.

STAGE 7:
BONNEVAL-SUR-ARC - COL DE L'ISERAN - VAL D'ISÈRE

Distance:	13 kilometres (8 miles)
Time:	$5^{1}/_{2}$-6 hours
Start altitude:	1787m (5863ft)
High point:	2764m (9068ft)
Low point:	1809m (5935ft)
Height gain:	977m (3205ft)
Height loss:	955m (3133ft)
Accommodation:	Val d'Isère - hotels + camping

The crossing of Col de l'Iseran marks a transition from the Maurienne to the Tarentaise. South of the col the River Arc collects the melt of various snowfields and glaciers of the massif, and drains clockwise round the Vanoise block, while north of the Iseran all streams flow into the Isère, a major tributary of the Rhône, in its counter-clockwise journey out of the mountains. East of Chambéry the Arc and Isère join forces, the two rivers effectively containing the Vanoise massif in their caliper-like embrace.

Col de l'Iseran is not only the lynchpin that connects the Maurienne and Tarentaise, it is also a symbol of two contrasting (and sometimes conflicting) styles of mountain usage. From Modane to the col the Tour of the Vanoise journeys through country largely unchallenged by the modern world. In the main refuges provide the only concession to tourist activity, the mountains remain for the most part unscarred. But from the summit of Col de l'Iseran to Val d'Isère, and beyond through Lac de Tignes and Val Claret, some of the hills and valleys have been sacrificed to the excesses of the winter ski industry. Pylons carrying cableways and ski tows march naked over the mountains, and broad bulldozed pistes have raped the hillsides. Yet sections of this desecrated land are contained within the Réserve Naturelle de Val d'Isère...

Happily this stage of the walk is not all gloom. Indeed, the first half of the day's route goes through as lovely a glen as any on the tour. Vallon de la Lenta is a delight of gentle pastures, old stone chalets, clear-running streams, a booming cascade - and magnificent views back to the south. There follows a climb through a gorge, the crossing of a snow bridge (Pont de la Neige), and steep grass slopes leading to the col. Col de l'Iseran is crossed by

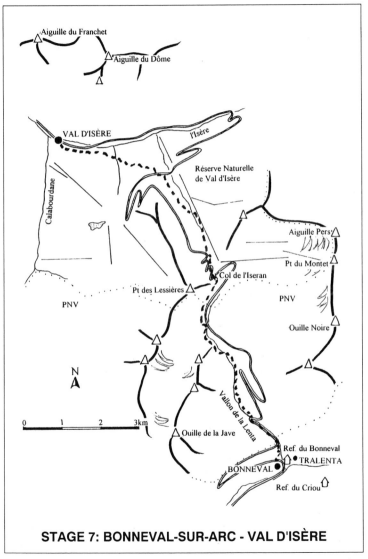

STAGE 7: BONNEVAL-SUR-ARC - VAL D'ISÈRE

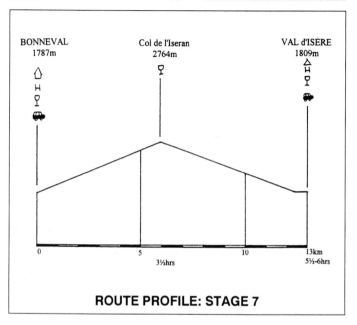

| BONNEVAL | Col de l'Iseran | VAL d'ISERE |
| 1787m | 2764m | 1809m |

ROUTE PROFILE: STAGE 7

road, and the descent on the northern side short-cuts a few hairpin bends before working a way down ski-slopes in the Vallon de l'Iseran. Then the trail turns away from the line of ski tows and gondola lifts to find a zigzag route down through forest to Val d'Isère. A challenging day, and a rewarding one.

*　　*　　*

A few paces north of the tourist information office at the north-eastern end of Bonneval in Tralenta, the GR5 is signposted along a service road heading to the right. This leads to the village's electricity generating plant where you bear left, now on a footpath which climbs steeply up a slope. At a crossing path turn left (the right-hand alternative crosses a torrent in a ravine). The way soon twists up the hillside keeping well to the left of the ravine, and with views onto Bonneval and through the valley becoming more extensive as height is gained. Come to a broad crossing track by a tunnel entrance, and

Pont de la Croé-Vie, where the climb begins to Col de la Vanoise
In normal summer conditions walkers cross the shallow Lac des
Vaches by a series of stepping-stones

Refuge de Péclet-Polset, lost in a wild landscape below Col de Chavière

Aiguille Doran, seen from Modane at the end of the Tour of the Vanoise

Vallon de la Lenta

continue uphill to the left of the tunnel. A small concrete shed is seen; keep left of this and climb on a trail that eventually reaches the Iseran road just above a stone-built hut.

Walk ahead along the road for about 1 kilometre (0.6 mile) until it curves sharply to the right over a bridge at **LA LENTA** (2140m: 7021ft 1hr). Immediately over the bridge bear left on a track and wander through the charming Vallon de la Lenta, a pastoral glen dotted with stone chalets and a fine waterfall bursting from a rocky cleft ahead. Five minutes along the track the way is joined by the high route alternative (GR5) from Bessans, which crosses a bridge from the left. Continue along the track, soon narrowing to a path that rises up the right-hand side of the cascades - superb views back through the glen to l'Albaron (3637m: 11,932ft) and La Grande Ciamarella (3676m: 12,060ft) and the fine-looking glaciers that form the main source of the Arc.

Above the cascades the trail crosses an enclosed pastureland before climbing to the road again at a hairpin bend by an abandoned three-storey building (2274m: 7461ft). Immediately leave the road and pass alongside the building where the trail divides. Take the right-hand option (the alternative merely goes to a vantage point) which winds into a small gorge and climbs from one grassy bluff to the next, each one providing spectacular views to the south. Eventually come to a natural snow bridge blocking the gorge, by which you cross to the left-hand (west) side. This *Pont de la Neige* is located some way below a road bridge; however the map shows the road bridge itself as the Pont de la Neige. If snow cover is poor, and conditions suggest the crossing to be unsafe, you will have to climb shaly slopes to the road, and continue from there.

The trail continues to climb through the gorge (beware falling stones) and briefly rejoins the road at the bridge (2528m: 8294ft).

Note: An alternative path cuts off left from the bridge near a stone shelter, and climbs into a glen whose upper reaches are only hinted at from below. A popular, and not difficult, ascent is made via this glen to the Pointe des Fours (3072m: 10,079ft) which tops the Glacier de la Jave. Although this cannot be seen from the Pont de la Neige road bridge, a good view may be had of it from the continuing path which leads to Col de l'Iseran.

Do not cross the road but continue along the left-hand side. At first the path edges the road, but soon begins to climb above it. At times the gradient is quite steep, and there are minor streams to cross. But the way is clear, though narrow in places, and eventually it strikes up a last steep grass slope to emerge on the **COL DE L'ISERAN** (2764m: 9068ft 3½hrs *refreshments*).

The col, the highest major road pass in the Alps, is marked by a huge cairn, a chapel (built in 1939, just three years after the road was opened) and an uninspiring building which houses the inevitable bar, snacks and souvenirs. Views are extensive, but not as satisfying as some of those enjoyed on the way from Bonneval, while traffic on the road comes as an unwelcome intrusion. The mountainscape ahead is somewhat dominated by ski machinery, while skiing continues through the summer on the Glacier du Grand Pisaillas above the col to the east.

Note: South-west of Col de l'Iseran the obvious sharp peak of Pointe des Lessières (3043m: 9984ft) provides a spectacular viewpoint. A

> route climbs directly to it from the col - sections of path, part-scrambling, one fixed rope section. See *Walking in the Tarentaise & Beaufortain Alps.*

Cross the road just below the building and take a waymarked path that rises a little to pass alongside a small stone hut, then descends north-westward, crossing the road two or three times before leaving it altogether by following down a scoop of hillside (the Vallon de l'Iseran) on the right-hand side of the road. The route is guided by a variety of pylons and some very large cairns, or stone pyramids.

Shortly before reaching a gondola lift station bear left to cross a torrent by footbridge. The trail then cuts through rough pastures, curves leftward and drops to the road. About 60 metres (65yds) along the road the continuing path descends on the right, soon giving views of Val d'Isère far below. La Tsanteleina (3602m: 11,818ft) and its neighbouring mountains that form the opposite wall of the valley to the north-east also contain the Italian frontier.

Cross steep grass- and shrub-covered slopes, then go through larch forest on a twisting path. There are several junctions in the forest, but the route to Val d'Isère is obvious. Near the bottom of the forest cross a footbridge over a torrent, and soon after this pass through a small hamlet, **LE LAISINANT** (1855m: 6086ft *camping*). Remaining on the south side of the valley the path leads directly into one of the major ski resorts in all the Alps.

VAL D'ISÈRE (1809m: 5935ft) *Hotels, camping (at Le Laisinant), restaurants, bars, shops, banks, PTT, bus service to Bourg-St-Maurice for SNCF trains. Tourist information: Office de Tourisme, 73155 Val d'Isère, Cedex (04 79 06 06 60). Lower-priced hotels: Le Relais du Ski (04 79 06 02 06); Foret (04 79 06 00 40); Epaule du Charvet (Pension) (04 79 06 00 04); Blanche Neige (04 79 06 04 02).*

*   *   *

Primarily a ski resort, and a fashionable one at that, Val d'Isère also attracts visitors in summer, and its shops, restaurants and bars enjoy a two-season trade, although a number of hotels are operational in winter only. The town's modern architecture largely follows traditional lines - unlike neighbouring Lac de Tignes and Val Claret - but there are plenty of signs of on-going expansion. In his guide to the Alps published pre-war, that great mountain connoisseur R.L.G. Irving listed Val d'Isère as the second of his favourite centres in the Graian Alps, giving as his criteria: "altitude, good quarters, green pastures, streams, flowers, and plenty of peaks to look at as well as to climb" (*The Alps*, published by Batsford, 1939). Of course, Irving was writing about a Val d'Isère that he would most likely find unrecognisable today, although much of his listed criteria remains good.

*   *   *

STAGE 8:
VAL D'ISÈRE - COL DE LA LEISSE - REFUGE DE LA LEISSE

Distance:	18 kilometres (11 miles)
Time:	6-6½ hours
Start altitude:	1809m (5935ft)
High point:	2758m (9049ft)
Low point:	2093m (6867ft)
Height gain:	1108m (3635ft)
Height loss:	430m (1411ft)
Accommodation:	Lac de Tignes (2hrs 15mins) - hotels
	Val Claret (2hrs 45mins) - hotels
	Refuge de la Leisse + camping

With two cols to cross (Pas de la Tovière and Col de la Leisse) between Val d'Isère and Refuge de la Leisse, it will be apparent that this stage which returns to the mountain wilderness can be quite challenging. However, having walked this far along the Tour of the Vanoise, and tackled steeper gradients than those demanded by either of these crossings, most trekkers will take it in their stride under normal conditions. But should snow still be lying the route will be made more arduous.

As with yesterday's stage, this section of the tour is split into two distinctive parts. The morning will be spent in view of either major ski resorts or their mechanical accoutrements (or both), while the second half leads into a landscape with more remote appeal. From Val d'Isère the way

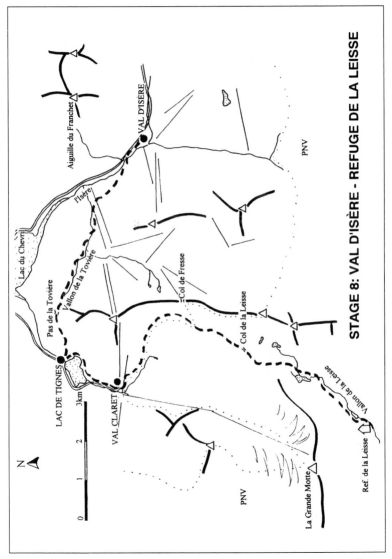

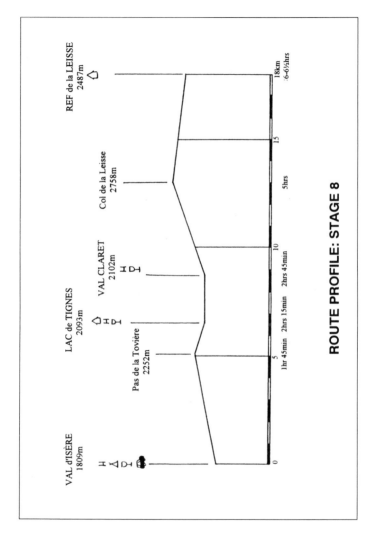

ROUTE PROFILE: STAGE 8

climbs through forest and along a gently-rising glen to the Pas de la Tovière where, if you're lucky, it's possible to see Mont Blanc in the distance. Then descent is made to the hideous ski resort of Lac de Tignes, but this is quickly passed on the way to Val Claret - an equally obtrusive resort of high-rise blocks.

Happily one soon loses sight of these on a trail that works a steady course south-east, then south-westward into an untamed land of big bold mountains, the highest of which is La Grande Motte, whose snowfields and glaciers shine like mirrors in the sun. La Grande Motte rises immediately above Col de la Leisse, its long south-westerly wall plunging into the glen in which the Refuge de la Leisse is found. Over Col de la Leisse the trail descends at a comfortable angle to moody tarns, screes and boulderscapes loud with the shrill cry of marmots.

From Val Claret to Modane our circuit follows the GR55, a high mountain alternative to the GR5, and a route that has been publicised in some quarters as a Traverse of the Vanoise, and even a Tour of the Vanoise. It forms a scenically varied and spectacular four-day section of our tour to match the grandeur experienced between Modane and Val d'Isère.

*   *   *

Walk through Val d'Isère along the main road (D.902) heading north-west toward La Daille and Tignes. On the outskirts of town, by a large building called L'Aigle Blanc, turn left on a minor road, cross the Isère river and immediately bear right on a track that curves left by a large electricity generating building. This becomes a forestry track, but in about three minutes leave it for a footpath branching to the right (GR5) signposted to Vallée Perdu and Les Sources. The trail winds pleasantly through larch forest, but when you pass beneath a ski tow, it suddenly climbs steeply to a crossing track with a parallel footpath.

Turn right along the path; contour across an open ski piste, then into larchwoods again. Rising out of the forest the way now crosses high rolling pastureland. After passing a large wooden cross and the ruins of the Chalet Superior de la Tovière, the trail leads into the lovely Vallon de la Tovière - a green and gentle glen walled on the left by Pointe du Lavachet (2696m: 8845ft), to the right by the crags of Roc de la Tovière, and with some handsome peaks hinted ahead.

The route through the Tovière glen is easy and undemanding.

One or two more ruins are passed before rising to the **PAS DE LA TOVIÈRE** (2252m: 7388ft 1hr 45mins), a broad grassy saddle littered with limestone rocks and patched with flowers. To the north the Italian side of Mont Blanc can be seen on a clear day, while deep below lies the dammed Lac du Chevril into which a large waterfall crashes its foam. Another glen, containing Lac de la Sassière, curves from the east below Aiguille de la Sassière and La Tsanteleina; this is the Grande Sassière Nature Reserve - a direct contrast to Lac de Tignes which will be seen in a few moments.

As the path continues, now descending westward, so the high-rise buildings of Lac de Tignes and Le Lavachet become visible in the valley below; a purpose-built ski resort whose architecture seems quite out of place, and whose cableways lace the mountainsides on both flanks of the valley. The trail leads directly down to the edge of the village. For our purposes it is unnecessary to go into Lac de Tignes, but should refreshment or overnight lodging be required, curve right just before reaching the lake.

LAC DE TIGNES (2093m: 6867ft 2hrs 15mins) *Hotels, gîte d'étape, bars, restaurants, shops, PTT. Cheapest accommodation: Gîte de Tignes (80 places, meals provided, manned July-August); Chalet-Hotel Lavachey (04 79 06 31 43); Le Gentiana (04 79 06 52 46); L'Albina (04 79 06 34 78).*

Instead of turning into the village follow a broad gravel path round the left-hand shore of the lake. At the far end bear left on another gravel path heading towards more monstrous high-rise buildings that comprise the ski resort of **VAL CLARET** (2102m: 6896ft 2hrs 45mins) *Hotels, shops, bars, bank. Cheapest hotels: de la Vanoise (04 79 06 31 90); le Curling (04 79 06 34 34).*

Continue beyond the high-rise blocks to a funicular station at the end of the road. Take a broad path on the left which rises on wood-braced steps towards more modern buildings. Near the head of the slope bear right on a path parallel with a chairlift. It swings to the right beneath the cables, then almost immediately a trail cuts off to the left. This is the one to take (GR55). The path soon forks. Take the left-hand option climbing across pastures. The waymarked trail rises steadily to pass through a cleft beside a tumbling stream, then over more open pastureland with the signpost on Col de Fresse seen on the walling

Refuge de la Leisse, owned by the PNV, can accommodate 48 in its dormitory

ridge above to the left. (Beyond that eastern ridgeline, and happily out of sight, is one of Europe's foremost ski playgrounds.)

The landscape becomes increasingly more barren as the trail re-enters the National Park and curves south-westward with the glacier-draped Grande Motte now dominating the view ahead. In poor visibility it will be necessary to keep alert to the cairns which guide the way to Col de la Leisse; when snow still covers the route in the early part of the season the ascent can be quite laborious, while later in the year the route should be obvious. The trail climbs over a series of false cols before finally topping **COL DE LA LEISSE** (2758m: 9049ft 5hrs).

There is no discernible descent at first, as the path goes through a trough before sloping down a series of natural steps in a wild, yet majestic land of raw scenery below the great cliffs of La Grande Motte. Lac des Nettes is passed on its eastern side, then you descend to the Plan des Nettes where the trail goes along the right-hand shore of another tarn, smaller than Lac des Nettes and with a tiny barrage at its southern outflow. The trail curves round towards the dam, then descends a short slope to the hut.

REFUGE DE LA LEISSE (2487m: 8159ft) *Owned by the PNV, 48 places, camping, meals provided, kitchen facilities, showers, guardian in summer (04 79 20 50 85), winter room permanently open.*

*　　　*　　　*

The refuge consists of three tent-shaped wooden buildings set on a natural terrace on the slopes of a bluff overlooking the Vallon de la Leisse. Toilet and washing facilities are meagre, but the outlook is very fine and the atmosphere easily created suits the impression of remoteness. Marmot and chamois are the hut's neighbours.

The southern wall of the glen marks the divide between that of La Leisse and the Vallon de la Rocheure. In that ridge wall, between the minor summits of Roc Blanc and Pierre Brune, Col de Pierre Blanche (2842m: 9324ft) provides a challenging route for walkers who might wish to explore the Rocheure glen and use Refuge de la Femma as a base. (But see Alternative Stage 9 below.)

*　　　*　　　*

STAGE 9:
REFUGE DE LA LEISSE - COL DE LA VANOISE - PRALOGNAN

Distance:	17 kilometres (10$^{1/}$2 miles)
Time:	6 hours
Start altitude:	2487m (8159ft)
High point:	2517m (8258ft)
Low point:	1418m (4652ft)
Height gain:	418m (1371ft)
Height loss:	1099m (3606ft)
Accommodation:	Refuge d'Entre Deux Eaux (1$^{1/}$2hrs + 20mins)
	Refuge du Col de la Vanoise (3$^{1/}$2hrs)
	Refuge les Barmettes (4hrs 45mins)
	Pralognan-la-Vanoise - hotels, gîtes d'étape + camping

The crossing of Col de la Vanoise to Pralognan is a classic stage, passing as

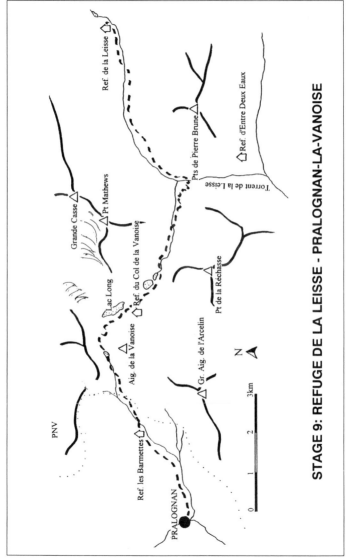

STAGE 9: REFUGE DE LA LEISSE - PRALOGNAN-LA-VANOISE

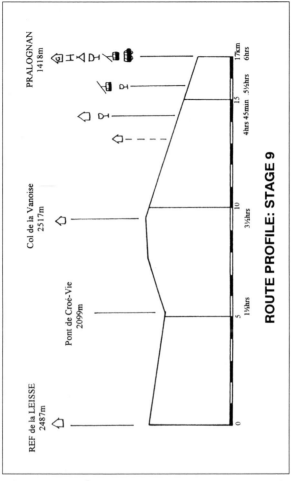

REF de la LEISSE
2487m

Pont de Croé-Vie
2099m

Col de la Vanoise
2517m

PRALOGNAN
1418m

ROUTE PROFILE: STAGE 9

it does from the sense of remoteness experienced at La Leisse, via the close proximity of high mountains on the col itself, to the 'fleshpots' of a resort village surrounded by lofty peaks. It forms an integral part of the shorter Tour of the Vanoise Glaciers (Tour des Glaciers de la Vanoise), and the final section in particular is extremely popular with all active (and semi-active) visitors to Pralognan, for whom no summer holiday in that village would be complete without spending at least one day climbing to the col and back again. It is, quite simply, one of the best-known of all walks in the Vanoise Alps.

The first part of this stage involves an easy descent through the Vallon de la Leisse to the humpbacked Pont de Croé-Vie, followed by a short climb to a high scoop of mountain country under the south-west flanks of La Grande Casse leading to the passage over Col de la Vanoise, and finally a steep and tiring descent to Pralognan which, as hinted above, will seldom be experienced in solitude.

Refuge de la Vanoise is the largest and busiest of all huts on the tour, and although it is reached rather early in the day, such is the splendour of its situation among glaciers, tarns, rock faces and soaring mountain peaks, that many trekkers choose to spend a night there. Should this be your decision, it should be possible to continue to Refuge de Péclet-Polset tomorrow (see Stage 10 for details).

With sufficient time at your disposal, an alternative would be to divert south from the main route at Pont de Croé-Vie as far as Refuge d'Entre

Below Refuge de la Leisse the trail crosses the glen's torrent on a wooden footbridge

Deux-Eaux, book in for the night there and spend the rest of the day exploring the Vallon de la Rocheure which cuts into the mountains behind it (roughly parallel to the Vallon de la Leisse). This gives an opportunity to unravel a little more of the geography of the area, and makes a superb, recommended 'rest day'. Details are given under Alternative Stage 9.

*   *   *

Back-track a short distance from Refuge de la Leisse, and then descend on a major signposted path sloping down into the lovely Leisse glen which, below the hut, is fairly flat-bottomed (watch for marmots, bouquetin and chamois). A footbridge takes the trail to the left bank of the stream, and the path remains there for the rest of the descent to Pont de Croé-Vie via a series of natural steps, and with several minor side streams that have to be crossed. Snowbanks often obscure the trail in places well into mid-summer, but numerous bootprints should ensure the route is well marked.

The valley makes a steady curve to the south, and as it does so a cascade is seen ahead, pouring from the cliffs walling the way to Col de la Vanoise. Above it La Grande Casse (Pointe Mathews) is seriously foreshortened, while looking behind, La Grande Motte appears quite a different mountain from the glacial giant that so dominated the view from Col de la Leisse.

Turning the bend in the valley familiar peaks are briefly shown down to the south-west; familiar from Stage 4 (l'Arpont to Plan du Lac). An attractive stone bridge spans the Torrent de la Leisse; this is **PONT DE CROÉ-VIE** (2099m: 6886ft 1¹/₂hrs), where you come to a junction of trails. Ours turns right to cross the bridge.

Note: The path which continues downvalley on the left bank goes directly (in 20 minutes) to **REFUGE D'ENTRE DEUX EAUX** (2120m: 6955ft) Privately-owned, 60 places, meals provided, kitchen facilities, showers, open summer only (04 79 20 50 85).

Cross the bridge and climb the zigzag path, initially among alpenroses, then becoming more stony as height is gained on the flanks of Pointe de la Réchasse. About 30 minutes from the bridge come to a trail junction (the left-hand path cuts across the mountainside

Pointe de la Grande Glière, from the Col de la Vanoise

and heads south to Refuge de l'Arpont). Continue ahead to pass a triangular memorial stone (2300m: 7546ft) erected in memory of two army officers who perished in the mountains. Just beyond this the path traverses a steep slope which, when snow-covered, is potentially dangerous and will demand care in tackling. Soon after you will see the remains of a wartime blockhouse on the right of the path.

The trail rises a little, then levels into an inner glen between Pointe de la Réchasse and La Grande Casse where the Vanoise stream flows parallel to the path on the right. Cross the stream on stepping stones and continue on its north bank. The glen, or trough, through which the route strikes north-westward is marshy in places (small tarns instead of marsh when winter snowbanks are melting), and as you progress so the huge screes fanning from the southern slopes of La Grande Casse create a barren scene. The trail recrosses the stream, and cairns lead across a stony plain to pass along the left-hand side of a small tarn (Lac du Col de la Vanoise). Climb a short grass step to overlook another tarn, Lac Rond, with the great slabs of Pointe de la Grande Glière and Aiguille de l'Epéna soaring ahead to the right, and the glaciers of La Grande Casse hanging above the far shore.

Lac des Vaches and La Grande Casse, highest of all Vanoise mountains

Now cross an open grassy plain to reach the rather ugly group of buildings of Refuge Félix Faure (named after a President of France who came here in 1897), better known as **REFUGE DU COL DE LA VANOISE** (2517m: 8258ft 3¹/₂hrs) *CAF-owned, 154 places, meals provided, kitchen facilities, guardian mid June to mid Sept (04 79 22 96 69), winter room permanently open.* Views from the hut are tremendous, dominated as they are by the powerful Grande Casse, below which lies yet another lake, Lac Long.

The descent trail to Pralognan passes the right-hand side of the refuge and skirts the deep bowl containing Lac Long, then zigzags west below the vast rock slabs of the Aiguille de la Vanoise. It's impossible to lose the way as the path (a mule track) is mostly broad and busy with walkers struggling up from Pralognan. Come to the shallow **LAC DES VACHES** (2319m: 7608ft 4hrs) which is crossed on stepping stones. From the south-western shore, where the Glière torrent pours out, another superb view is afforded back to La Grande Casse, while the deep, deep valley ahead provides a hint that the remainder of the descent will be a strain on the knees.

Note: A few minutes below the lake an alternative trail cuts off to the right, and in about 30 minutes climbs up to Col Rosset - magnificent views.

Continue down towards the valley. The main trail is a broad and stony track, but there are several minor paths, all more or less steep and twisting among marmot burrows and low-growing shrubs. Then the main trail is contained between drystone walls, and soon after you cross the stream, leave the National Park once more and come to **REFUGE LES BARMETTES** (2030m: 6660ft 4hrs 45mins) *Privately-owned, 22 places, meals provided, bar, restaurant service, open in summer only (04 79 08 75 64).*

The broad track continues to wind down the mountainside heading south-west. On coming to a junction of tracks by a building on the edge of forest, take the right-hand option signposted to Les Fontanettes. Cutting through forest the trail soon reaches a car park, chairlift, and a road at **LES FONTANETTES** (1644m: 5394ft 5¹/₂hrs *refreshments*). Immediately beyond a bar-restaurant, bear left on a footpath descending past a few stone chalets. This comes onto the road again at a hairpin bend. Go round the hairpin, then break away left on the continuing path which enters forest once more and twists its way down to a small chapel, water fountain and a cobbled alley leading into the main street of Pralognan.

PRALOGNAN-LA-VANOISE (1418m: 4652ft) *Hotels, gîtes d'étape, camping, shops, restaurants, bars, bank, PTT. Tourist information & refuge booking service: Office de Tourisme, 73710 Pralognan-la-Vanoise (04 79 08 79 08). Gîtes d'étape: La Chèverie (30 places) (04 79 08 72 59); Maison du Randonneur (24 places) (04 79 08 71 54); Le Petit Mont-Blanc (37 places) (04 79 08 72 73); Isertan Chalet-Refuge (70 places) (04 79 08 73 11). Lower-priced hotels: Le Parisien (04 79 08 72 31); Le Vallée Blanche (04 79 08 70 74); de la Vanoise (04 79 08 70 34).*

*   *   *

Pralognan is an attractive small resort hemmed in by crowding mountains and with all services likely to be needed by walkers seeking an overnight stay. To the south-east any onward progress at first appears to be blocked by the soaring walls of the Grand Marchet and Roc de la Vallette, but the valley sneaks below these among forests, as tomorrow's route will prove. Although it has some skiing potential on both sides of the valley, Pralognan has largely escaped the architectural vandalism that has swamped many French ski resorts, and the close proximity of the National Park has effectively limited any opportunities for expansion. As a summer resort it has undoubted appeal, and attracts mountaineers, mountain walkers and general tourists in great numbers. In July and August especially accommodation is likely to be at a premium, so if you intend to stay there during this peak season, it will be worth booking ahead. Buses link Pralognan with the 'outside world' at Moutiers, which has SNCF railway station.

The Office de Tourisme is located in the middle of the village fronting the main street on the west side.

* * *

ALTERNATIVE STAGE 9:
REFUGE DE LA LEISSE - REFUGE D'ENTRE DEUX EAUX - REFUGE DE LA FEMMA - REFUGE D'ENTRE DEUX EAUX

Distance:	21 kilometres (13 miles)
Time:	6 hours
Start altitude:	2487m (8159ft)
High point:	2323m (7621ft)
Low point:	2053m (6736ft)
Height gain:	337m (1106ft)
Height loss:	704m (2310ft)
Accommodation:	Refuge d'Entre Deux Eaux (1hr 50mins)
	Refuge de la Femma (4hrs) - + camping

Trekkers with sufficient days in hand are urged to consider this alternative; a 'day off' from the main tour which gives an opportunity to enjoy a few hours of walking without a heavy rucksack through a delightful glen easily accessible from Refuge d'Entre Deux Eaux, which in itself is only 20 minutes away from the continuing route. The idea here is to go down through the Vallon de la Leisse on the Col de la Vanoise trail, then branch off at Pont de Croé-Vie as far as Entre Deux Eaux; arrange a night's accommodation at the

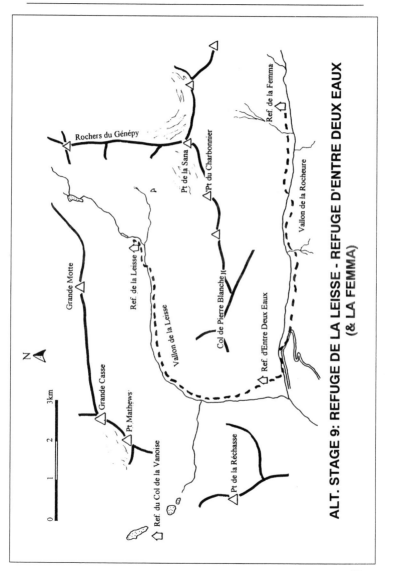

ALT. STAGE 9: REFUGE DE LA LEISSE - REFUGE D'ENTRE DEUX EAUX (& LA FEMMA)

private refuge there and, leaving your rucksack behind, wander through the Vallon de la Rocheure to Refuge de la Femma. After a drink, or lunch, at La Femma (a splendid PNV hut), return to Entre Deux Eaux for the night, and next day resume the Tour of the Vanoise as far as Pralognan.

There are many good things in favour of such a plan. For a start it is pleasant to have a rest from carrying a full rucksack for a day midway through a long tour, and although there's quite a lot of ground to cover, the walking is for the most part easy and undemanding. Refuge d'Entre Deux Eaux has a fine situation. A one-time dairy farm, there's a charming atmosphere to be found there, while purpose-built Refuge de la Femma is no less atmospheric and will surely tempt all visitors to return again to spend at least one night there on another occasion. As for the lovely Rocheure glen, few could fail to be enchanted by it - wild flowers colour the pastures, the stream is at one time a gentle meandering flow, then a bullying torrent carving mini-gorges in the valley bed. And views to the Glaciers de la Vanoise seen on the return walk are magnificent.

*   *   *

Follow directions as for Stage 9 through the Vallon de la Leisse as far as the trail junction at **PONT DE CROÉ-VIE** (2099m: 6886ft 1¹/₂hrs), but instead of crossing the bridge continue along the trail which remains on the left bank of the La Leisse torrent, now carving a way through a minor gorge. At a signposted path junction bear left and come to **REFUGE D'ENTRE DEUX EAUX** (2120m: 6955ft 1hr 50mins) *Privately owned, 60 places, meals provided, kitchen facilities, showers, open summer only (04 79 20 50 85).* It is advisable to arrange accommodation for the night here before continuing to La Femma.

Continue down the track which leads beyond the refuge, and cross the Torrent de la Rocheure on a wooden bridge. Bear left immediately on a narrow trail that soon becomes rather vague as it climbs among alpenroses, then emerges onto a tarmac road. Wander up the road for a little over 1 kilometre (0.6 mile). Just after passing an old stone farm building the road makes a hairpin to the right at an altitude of 2200m (7218ft), with a track striking ahead through the Vallon de la Rocheure.

Walk ahead along the track as it winds between undulating pastures, crosses to the north bank of the stream, and soon ends at the

CHALET DE LA ROCHEURE (3½hrs). A footpath continues over more pastures towards the head of the glen, while off to the right a cirque topped by the Pointes du Châtelard looks very enticing. The trail crosses a side stream and moments later arrives at the refuge.

REFUGE DE LA FEMMA (2323m: 7621ft 4hrs) *Owned by the PNV, 48 places, camping, meals provided, kitchen facilities, showers, guardian in summer (04 79 20 50 85). Winter room permanently open.* The timber-built refuge stands three storeys high, with two adjacent buildings along the same lines as those at La Leisse, and enjoys fine views downvalley to the west.

An alternative route climbs north then west from here to cross Col de Pierre Blanche (2842m: 9324ft), from which Refuge de la Leisse is gained. At the head of the valley beyond La Femma, Col de la Rocheure provides strenuous ways of cutting over the mountains to Pont de la Neige on the route to Col de l'Iseran, or to Val d'Isère via the Calabourdane glen.

Return to Refuge d'Entre Deux Eaux by retracing your steps through the Rocheure glen. Allow 1½-2 hours for this.

*   *   *

To resume with the Tour of the Vanoise next day, wander back upvalley from Entre Deux Eaux as far as Pont de Croé-Vie and rejoin the route to Col de la Vanoise and Pralognan as described under Stage 9. Allow 4½-5 hours for this.

*   *   *

STAGE 10:
PRALOGNAN - REFUGE DE PÉCLET-POLSET

Distance:	12 kilometres (7½ miles)
Time:	4-4½ hours
Start altitude:	1418m (4652ft)
High point:	2474m (8117ft)
Height gain:	1056m (3465ft)
Accommodation:	Les Prioux (1hr 10mins) - Chalet-Refuge Le Repoju
	Refuge de Péclet-Polset

STAGE 10: PRALOGNAN - REFUGE PÉCLET-POLSET

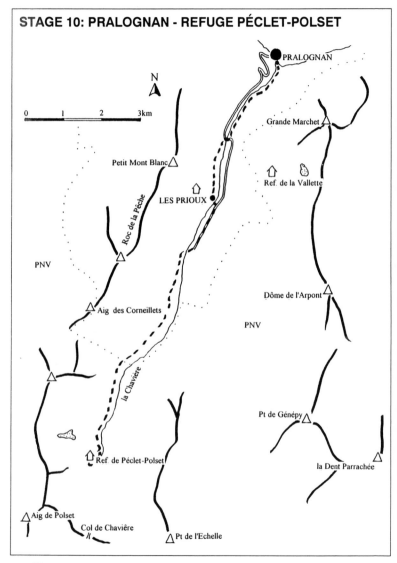

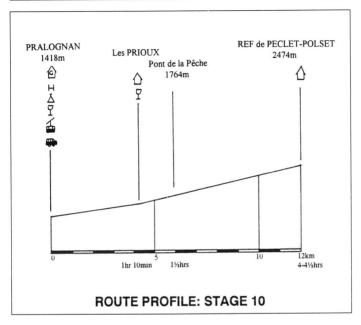

ROUTE PROFILE: STAGE 10

This is a fairly undemanding stage, despite the amount of height gain, and if need be under good conditions fit mountain walkers should be able to continue beyond Péclet-Polset, cross Col de Chavière and descend to Refuge de l'Orgère (an 8 hour day, plus rest stops) or even continue as far as Modane in 9$^{1/2}$ hours for the super-fit or anxious. However, it would be a shame to do so, for the wild landscapes around the refuge need contemplation; there's a lake to visit and the rough grandeur of this northern side of the Polset-Echelle ridge system to absorb before making the final crossing to the Maurienne and the homeward journey.

But it would be wrong to assume, from the above paragraph, that the valley leading from Pralognan to Péclet-Polset is all wild and untamed. It's not. Much of the way leads through pastoral countryside, with forest and meadows lower down, and broad pastures and occasional farms at mid-height. The gradient is for the most part generous, with few steep sections to contend with. And above the large car parking area at Pont de la Pêche, the trail is likely to be busy in high season with day visitors wandering to the hut

87

for lunch before returning to more homely surroundings in the late afternoon.

*　　　*　　　*

Leave Pralognan at the southern end of the village, heading along a road beside Hotel de la Vanoise. It soon veers right and crosses a tributary of the Doron de Chavière river. Bear left on a minor road and pass the municipal campsite, then veer right and walk through the large Isertan campsite (note the Isertan Chalet-Refuge as you wander through). The campsite road curves left near the river and soon after a footpath / track breaks off to the right. Follow this into the Isertan forest. In 15 minutes from leaving the centre of Pralognan pass the Pont de Chollière off to your right, and continue on the east bank of the river. The track narrows to a footpath rising steadily through the forest.

In another half-hour come to the road at **PONT DE GERLAN** (1592m: 5223ft 45mins). Cross the bridge and immediately turn left on a track and in a few paces pass a public toilet block. The track rises gently through meadows on the west bank of the Doron de Chavière, with two paths striking off for the ascent of the popular Petit Mont Blanc (2677m: 8783ft) named, not because of any resemblance to the Monarch of the Alps, but on account of the chalk-white gypsum exposed near the summit.

The track leads directly to the hamlet of **LES PRIOUX** (1hr 10mins) accommodation and refreshments: *Chalet-Refuge Le Repoju, privately-owned, 24 beds, meals provided (04 79 08 73 79)*. Walk through the hamlet and onto the road, and continue upvalley.

Note: A path cuts off left here and climbs to the Chalet des Nants, from which two options are available. One bears left to Refuge de la Vallette, the other traverses right and is used by some trekkers on the shorter Tour des Glaciers de la Vanoise to gain Col d'Aussois and Refuge Fond d'Aussois. This latter option makes for a very long day.

Remain on the road as far as a large parking area. Just beyond the car park branch right on a track to cross the river again at **PONT DE LA PÊCHE** (1764m: 5787ft). The track winds uphill above a small gorge and comes to the little chapel of la Motte before curving right and leading through pastures with good views ahead. Drawing level with the alp of Ritort, about an hour from Pont de la Pêche, the track forks.

Note: The left branch entices with a route across the river again to Alp Ritort, and continues beyond the buildings to climb steeply before reaching the trail from Chalet des Nants (see above) which crosses Col d'Aussois for an alternative route to Refuge du Fond d'Aussois (6hrs from Ritort).

The Péclet-Polset trail remains on the west bank. About 15 minutes later come to another trail junction. This time the alternative (right-hand) option breaks away to Col Rouge and Refuge du Saut on a cross-country route to the ski resort of Méribel.

The track maintains a steady gradient, passes a stone building and a roofless ruin, curves into a grassy combe, then climbs by way of zigzags into a wilder region overlooked by the Aiguille de Polset and Pointe de l'Echelle. A short path spur off to the right leads directly to the hut.

REFUGE DE PÉCLET-POLSET (2474m: 8117ft) *CAF-owned, 80 places, meals provided, kitchen facilities, guardian mid June to mid Sept (04 79 08 72 13), winter room permanently open.*

*   *   *

Of all the huts visited on the Tour of the Vanoise, Péclet-Polset enjoys the wildest aspect, especially early in the season when plenty of snow still lies round about. South of the refuge a stony amphitheatre dotted with small pools and tarns, often with little iceflows in them, is walled by raw peaks and ridges from which old snowfields, small glaciers or scree slopes present a gloomy picture when dark clouds conceal the sun.

North-west of the hut lies Lac Blanc, its milky-blue waters fed by numerous rivulets draining from the Glacier de Gebroulaz, while the twin aiguilles of Péclet and Polset rise from a long line of cliffs behind it. A short walk from the hut leads to Lac Blanc and is highly recommended.

*   *   *

STAGE 11:
REFUGE DE PÉCLET-POLSET - COL DE CHAVIÈRE - MODANE

Distance:	14 kilometres (8$^{1}/_{2}$ miles)
Time:	5$^{1}/_{2}$ hours
Start altitude:	2474m (8117ft)
High point:	2796m (9173ft)
Low point:	1058m (3471ft)
Height gain:	322m (1056ft)
Height loss:	1738m (5702ft)
Accommodation:	Refuge de l'Orgère (alt. route - 3$^{1}/_{2}$hrs)
	Refuge de l'Aiguille Doran (alt. route - 3hrs 45mins) + camping
	Modane - hotels + camping

Col de Chavière is the highest pass crossed by any Grande Randonnée route, but taken from Refuge de Péclet-Polset there are no reasons to feel intimidated by this. Seen from just above the hut the saddle is an obvious one, and it appears tantalisingly close. In good conditions, with clear visibility and no soft snowfields to labour through, it can be reached in a little over an hour and a quarter, the final steep climb making a rightful demand for such a pass. However, in poor visibility the route calls for due respect and concentration, while an electrical storm makes this a crossing to avoid at all costs.

Descent to Modane offers a choice of two routes, the trail dividing about 45 minutes below the col. The standard route taken by GR55 veers to the right of the lump of Tête Noire and curves anti-clockwise below the south-western cliffline, while the alternative cuts along the eastern flank of Tête Noire above the Orgère glen before making a sudden steep descent to the refuge, then joining GR5 for the final downhill trudge through forest shared by GR55. Both routes have their advocates. The main GR55 trail is, perhaps, slightly less demanding than the alternative, while trekkers on the Orgère route are more likely to catch sight of wildlife, and also have an opportunity to stop off at the refuge for refreshment.

One last thought before decisions are made: it is quite probable that you need to begin the journey home tomorrow. If so you may welcome prospects of a night in a hotel bed in Modane with the opportunity to start your journey afresh in the morning. Alternatively, return to 'civilisation' may be something

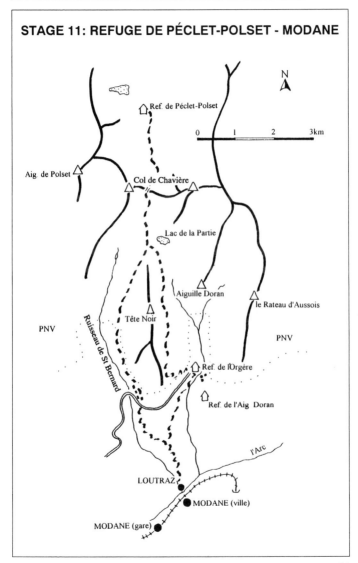

STAGE 11: REFUGE DE PÉCLET-POLSET - MODANE

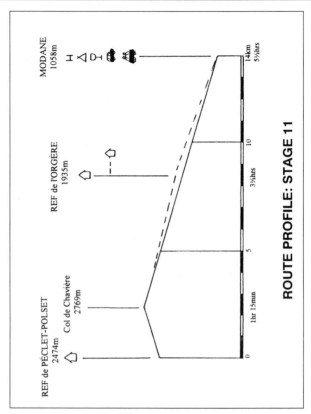

ROUTE PROFILE: STAGE 11

you wish to put off as long as possible. In which case you may be tempted to spend a last night in the sanctity of the mountains. Those so tempted have a choice of refuges for overnight accommodation - l'Orgère or Aiguille Doran. There will still be time to descend to Modane after breakfast for the train home. The choice is yours!

*   *   *

Leaving the hut either walk back along the path spur heading east to rejoin the main GR55 trail, or take a path going west immediately behind the hut, then veering left (south) across and through a band of rocks to find the main trail near a pool. The way rises southward below the cliffs of Dôme de Polset with the rocky Col de Chavière clearly seen ahead. Snow patches lie throughout most of the summer in the basin below the col where rocky islands jut out here and there. The route is obvious unless the mist is down; in such cases concentration will be required to follow a sporadic line of cairns.

The final ascent is up scree, then along a steeply sloping ramp of unstable grit that makes a pathway up the north-facing crags. Early in the season beware of ice.

COL DE CHAVIÈRE (2796m: 9173ft 1hr 15mins) is not only the highest point on the Tour of the Vanoise, but is without question the finest true col of the circuit; a narrow saddle in a rocky crest that plunges to both north and south. The col is marked by a large cairn, and on the proverbial clear day views are said to be extensive. Mont Blanc should be evident to the north-east, while looking south-west Mont Thabor and major summits of the Écrins Massif jostle for attention.

Looking south the trail divide below the block of Tête Noire is obvious. The right-hand path is the main GR55, that which skirts leftwards round the eastern flank of the block is the Orgère alternative.

Cairns lead the route down from the col. At first on scree (care required) slanting leftward into a basin, keep to the right of a spur, then over a broad open plateau with the Lac de la Partie seen below to the left. Midway across this plateau a faint trail (not shown on the D&R map) cuts off left going down to the tarn and on to Col du Ravin Noir. Ignore this and continue ahead for a further 5 minutes, and at the southern end of the plateau, about 45 minutes from the col, come to the main trail junction marked by a signpost. The right-hand path goes directly to Modane by way of Polset; the left-hand option leads to Refuge de l'Orgère, Refuge de l'Aiguille Doran and, via GR5, to Modane.

Main route (GR55): Skirting the right-hand side of Tête Noire the path slopes quite steeply down to cross the so-called Grand Planay, loses more height and enters forest above the left bank of the Ruisseau de St Bernard. Passing below a line of cliffs the trail leads to the few buildings of **POLSET** (1840m: 6037ft 3¹/₂hrs). A track continues the descent to a narrow road (D106, which leads from Freney to l'Orgère).

Cross the road and follow a mule-trail heading down through forest to **MODANE.**

Alternative route via l'Orgère: The left-hand trail makes an undemanding traverse of the east flank of Tête Noire, descending gradually except on rare occasions, until coming to the southern end of the Tête Noire spur where it suddenly swoops down in tight twists through forest, and leads directly to **REFUGE DE L'ORGÈRE** (1935m: 6348ft 3^{1}/$_{2}$hrs) *PNV-owned, 56 places, meals provided, kitchen facilities, showers; guardian 15 June-15 Sept (04 79 05 11 65), winter room permanently open.*

Note: Should you plan to spend a last night instead at Refuge de l'Aiguille Doran, descend the pastures below the Orgère refuge, cross the stream and turn right on a track leading to the few stone chalets of Orgère, and continue down the stony track for another 300 metres to find **REFUGE DE L'AIGUILLE DORAN** (1860m: 6102ft 3hrs 45mins) *Privately-owned, 40 places, camping, meals provided, showers; open 15 May-15 Oct (04 72 12 58 70).*

Descent route, l'Orgère to Modane: This section of the descent reverses the upward route followed on Stage 1. Walk down the road for a very short distance to find a signpost directing the GR5 path down through forest. The way is clear and obvious, with signs at all trail junctions where any doubt might otherwise occur. Allow 1^{1}/$_{2}$-2 hours.

MODANE (1058m: 3471ft) *Hotels, camping, restaurants, shops, banks, PTT, railway link with Chambéry. Tourist information: Office de Tourisme, 73500 Modane (04 79 05 22 35). Hotels: du Commerce (04 79 05 00 78); de France (04 79 05 23 46); des Voyageurs (04 70 05 01 39); le Perce-Neige (04 79 05 00 50).*

*   *   *

Route Summary

Route	Dist.	Ht. gain	Time	Page
1: Modane-Ref de l'Orgère	5.5km	877m	2¹/₂-3hrs	26
2: Ref de l'Orgère-Col du Barbier- Ref du Plan Sec	11km	574m	4¹/₂hrs	32
3: Ref du Plan Sec-Ref de l'Arpont	18km	486m	5¹/₂-6hrs	37
4: Ref de l'Arpont-Ref du Plan du Lac	12km	624m	5hrs	43
5: Ref du Plan du Lac-Ref du Cuchet- Ref du Vallonbrun	18km	448m	6hrs	50
6: Ref du Vallonbrun-Bessans-Bonneval	16km	141m	4¹/₂hrs	56
7: Bonneval-Col de l'Iseran-Val d'Isère	13km	977m	5¹/₂-6hrs	62
8: Val d'Isère-Col de la Leisse- Ref de la Leisse	18km	1108m	6-6¹/₂hrs	68
9: Ref de la Leisse-Col de la Vanoise- Pralognan	17km	418m	6hrs	74
A9: Ref de la Leisse-Ref d'Entre Deux Eaux- Ref de la Femma-Ref d'Entre Deux Eaux	21km	337m	6hrs	82
10: Pralognan-Ref de Péclet-Polset	12km	1056m	4-4¹/₂hrs	85
11: Ref de Péclet-Polset-Col de Chavière- Modane	14km	322m	5¹/₂hrs	90

*   *   *

Short Tours in the Vanoise

Walkers unable, or unwilling, to commit themselves to the full Tour of the Vanoise are fortunate in being able to break the route into two smaller circuits using the Doron gorge as the geographical divider. The first involves a circular route round the main glacier block at the western end of the ToV, the second concentrates on the eastern half. Both are outlined below, while a third option is to make a north-south crossing of the best of the region from the Tarentaise to the Maurienne. This Traverse of the Vanoise is also briefly described.

*　　*　　*

TOUR DES GLACIERS DE LA VANOISE

If Modane is taken as the starting point for this shorter tour, the circuit can be achieved in five or six days by adopting stages similar to those of the main tour. If, however, Pralognan is to be used as an initial base, the 'official' Tour des Glaciers, as publicised locally, may be followed in only four days, with three overnights in huts along the way.

*

i: First of all the Tour des Glaciers de la Vanoise starting from Modane.

Stage 1: **MODANE - REFUGE DE L'ORGÈRE** - 2^{1}/$_{2}$-3 hours

Stage 2: **REFUGE DE L'ORGÈRE - REFUGE DU PLAN SEC -**
4^{1}/$_{2}$ hours

Stage 3: **REFUGE DU PLAN SEC - REFUGE DE L'ARPONT -**
5^{1}/$_{2}$-6 hours

Stage 4: **REFUGE DE L'ARPONT - REFUGE DU COL DE LA**

VANOISE - 5 hours
Route: Follow the main ToV upvalley from l'Arpont to the trail junction above the northern end of the Doron gorge (2hrs 45mins), then break away on the left-hand trail to traverse the east flank of Pointe de la Réchasse, joining the main trail to Col de la Vanoise as described under Stage 9.

Stage 5: **REFUGE DU COL DE LA VANOISE - REFUGE DE PÉCLET-POLSET - VIA PRALOGNAN** - 6^{1}/$_{2}$-7 hours

Stage 6: **REFUGE DE PÉCLET-POLSET - MODANE** - 5^{1}/$_{2}$ hours

*

ii: Starting from Pralognan the 'official' Tour des Glaciers de la Vanoise follows the route outlined below.

Stage 1: **PRALOGNAN - REFUGE DE LA VALLETTE** - 4^{1}/$_{2}$-5 hours
Route: Leave Pralognan as described in Stage 10, but as the road linking the municipal campsite with the Isertan campsite curves right, leave it for a path ahead which climbs steeply through the Isertan forest to gain the Pas de l'Âne by a rough scramble. Continue to the Roc du Tambour, after which the gradient eases on the final approach to the **REFUGE DE LA VALLETTE** (2584m: 8478ft) *PNV-owned, 45 places, meals provided, kitchen facilities, guardian in summer (04 79 22 96 38), winter room permanently open.*

Stage 2: **REFUGE DE LA VALLETTE - REFUGE DU FOND D'AUSSOIS** - 7^{1}/$_{2}$ hours
Route: A strenuous crossing of 2916m (9567ft) Col d'Aussois, the day begins easy enough by descending 400m (1312ft) to the Chalet des Nants, traverses south-west to Montaimont, then climbs to the Cirque du Génépy. The way climbs steeply to another belvedere trail to be joined by a path rising from Alp Ritort. From here the route now heads south-east up the glen of the Rosoire stream, before breaking off southward with a final sharp ascent to the col. Over this the descent is quite tiring before grass slopes lead to the

REFUGE DU FOND D'AUSSOIS (2324m: 7625ft) *CAF-owned, 40 places, camping, meals provided, kitchen facilities, guardian July & August (04 79 20 39 83). Winter room permanently open.*

Stage 3: **REFUGE DU FOND D'AUSSOIS - REFUGE DE L'ARPONT** - 6-6¹/₂ hours
Route: From Fond d'Aussois to Refuge du Plan Sec will take little more than an hour. Thereafter the route is the same as that described as Stage 3 of the main ToV.

Stage 4: **REFUGE DE L'ARPONT - PRALOGNAN - VIA COL DE LA VANOISE** - 7-7¹/₂ hours

Note: Pralognan-la-Vanoise may be reached by public transport via rail to Moutiers (on the line Chambéry-Bourg St Maurice), and bus from there.

*   *   *

TOUR OF THE EASTERN VANOISE

This five-day circuit begins and ends at Refuge du Plan du Lac, that fine PNV hut with its lovely view across the unseen Doron gorge to the Glaciers de la Vanoise. Plan du Lac is reached by the shuttle bus service from Termignon, the *navette*. From the railway station at Modane take the bus to Termignon. The shuttle bus stop (*Arrêt Navette*) is located at the western end of the village near a butcher's shop.

As for the route of this tour it follows each of the stages of the main ToV from Stage 5 to Stage 8 inclusive, then adopts part of Alternative Stage 9 as far as the Torrent de la Rocheure below Entre Deux Eaux.

Stage 1: **REFUGE DU PLAN DU LAC - REFUGE DU VALLONBRUN** - 6 hours

Stage 2: **REFUGE DU VALLONBRUN - BONNEVAL-SUR-ARC -** 4¹/₂ hours

Stage 3: **BONNEVAL - COL DE L'ISERAN - VAL D'ISÈRE** - 5^{1}/$_{2}$-6 hours

Stage 4: **VAL D'ISÈRE - COL DE LA LEISSE - REFUGE DE LA LEISSE** - 6-6^{1}/$_{2}$ hours

Stage 5: **REFUGE DE LA LEISSE - REFUGE DU PLAN DU LAC -** 3^{1}/$_{2}$ hours
Route: Take Alternative Stage 9 beyond Refuge d'Entre Deux Eaux to the bridge crossing the Torrent de la Rocheure, and over this follow the final part of the route described to Plan du Lac as per Stage 4 of the main ToV.

*   *   *

TRAVERSE OF THE VANOISE

By combining the GR5 with GR55, a five-day crossing can be achieved. Unlike the previously-described tours, this is a linear route, one of the highlights of the 660 kilometre (400 miles) *Grande Traversée des Alpes*, the full extent of which will take at least four weeks of trekking. (See *Walking the French Alps: GR5*.) For this Traverse of the Vanoise walkers will need to make for Landry in the Isère valley which separates the Tarentaise from the Beaufortain Alps. The valley is served by rail (Chambéry-Bourg St Maurice line) with a station at Landry.

Stage 1: **LANDRY - REFUGE DU COL DU PALET** - 7 hours
Route: This is a long valley route cutting roughly south-east of Landry along the Ponturin river, with an option of reducing the walk by 1^{1}/$_{2}$ hours by taking a bus as far as Peisey-Nancroix; or of stopping at an alternative PNV refuge, Porte du Rosuel, after 3 hours. The full walk continues upvalley beyond Rosuel, rising steadily towards Col du Palet in the valley headwall. The hut is reached about 10 minutes before the col. **REFUGE DU COL DU PALET** (2556m: 8386ft) *PNV-owned, 48 places, meals provided, kitchen facilities, guardian from June to mid Sept (04 79 07 91 47). Winter room permanently open.*

Stage 2: **REFUGE DU COL DU PALET - COL DU PALET - COL DE LA LEISSE - REFUGE DE LA LEISSE** - 4$^1/_2$ hours
Route: Continuing along the GR5 the trail crosses Col du Palet and descends towards Lac de Tignes, but when the track forks bear right and slope down to Val Claret and there join GR55 and the main ToV route described under Stage 8. A fine day's walking. Thereafter the traverse follows the Tour of the Vanoise as below.

Stage 3: **REFUGE DE LA LEISSE - COL DE LA VANOISE - PRALOGNAN** - 6 hours

Stage 4: **PRALOGNAN - REFUGE DE PÉCLET-POLSET** - 4-4$^1/_2$ hours

Stage 5: **REFUGE DE PÉCLET-POLSET - COL DE CHAVIÈRE - MODANE** - 5$^1/_2$ hours

*　　　*　　　*

Appendices

APPENDIX A:
USEFUL ADDRESSES

1: Tourist Information:

French Government Tourist Office
178 Piccadilly
London W1V 0AL
(0171 629 2869)

French Government Tourist Office
610 Fifth Avenue
New York
NY 10020-2452

French State Railways
179 Piccadilly
London W1V 0BA

In France:

Agence Touristique Départmentale de
   la Savoie
24 boulevard de la Colonne
73000 Chambéry

Parc National de la Vanoise
135 rue du Docteur Julliand
BP 705
737007 Chambéry cedex

Office de Tourisme
73480 Bessans

Office de Tourisme
73480 Bonneval-sur-Arc

Office de Tourisme
73500 Modane

Office de Tourisme
73710 Pralognan-la-Vanoise

Office de Tourisme
73320 Tignes

Office de Tourisme
73150 Val d'Isère

2: Friends of the National Park & French Alpine Club:

Amis du Parc National de la Vanoise
PB 705
73000 Chambéry
France

Club Alpin Français
24 avénue de la Laumière
75019 Paris
France

3: Map Suppliers:

Edward Stanford Ltd
12-14 Long Acre
London WC2E 9BR
(0171 836 1321)

The Map Shop
15 High Street
Upton-upon-Severn
Worcs. WR8 0HJ

Rand McNally Map Store
10 East 53rd Street
New York
NY

IGN Shop
107 rue la Baetie
75008 Paris
France

*   *   *

APPENDIX B:
REFUGE RESERVATION

Below is a sample letter in French which may help when making reservations in advance for refuge accommodation. As mentioned in the Introduction a central reservation facility exists for walkers planning to stay in refuges in the Vanoise region during July and August. There is a charge for this service based on the number of bedspaces required each night.

Days of the week, in French, are:
dimanche (Sunday); *lundi* (Monday); *mardi* (Tuesday); *mercredi* (Wednesday); *jeudi* (Thursday); *vendredi* (Friday); *samedi* (Saturday)

July is *juillet*; August is *août*

*

NAME & ADDRESS   Centrale de Réservation
(BLOCK CAPITALS)   Maison du Parc et Tourisme
                                  73710 Pralognan-la-Vanoise
                                  France

Date

Dear Sir/Madam,

I am planning a walking tour of the Vanoise mountains during July ([and] August) and would like to reserve a bed (....beds) for one person (....persons) at the following refuges. I (we) wish to have half-pension at each refuge.

Day & date	*Refuge*
Monday 30 July	de l'Orgère
Tuesday 31 July	Plan Sec
Wednesday 1 August	l'Arpont

I enclose an International Reply Coupon for your response, and thank you for your assistance.

Yours faithfully

NAME & ADDRESS   Centrale de Réservation
(BLOCK CAPITALS)   Maison du Parc et du Tourisme
                           73710 Pralognan-la-Vanoise
                           France

Date

Monsieur/Madame,

Pendant les mois de juillet ([et] d'août) j'ai l'intention de faire un tour de la Vanoise en suivant les randonnées pédestres.

Je voudrais réserver un lit (...lits) pour une personne (...personnes) aux refuges suivants. Je voudrais prendre demi-pension à chaque refuge.

Jour et date	*Refuge*
lundi 30 juillet	de l'Orgère
mardi 31 juillet	Plan Sec
mercredi 1 aout	l'Arpont

Veuillez trouver ci-joint un coupon-réponse international.

En vous remerciant d'avance, je vous prie d'agréer, Monsieur, l'expression de mes sentiments distingués.

Signature

*   *   *

Surprisingly, little has been written about the Graian Alps, which includes the Vanoise, so the literature is sparse. A few accounts of mountaineering ascents appear in various journals, and on occasion an article appears in the outdoor press of interest to walkers, but little in comparison with certain other alpine regions. However, the following books contain material that is both informative and entertaining for walkers planning a visit to this delightful range.

* *Walking in the Tarentaise & Beaufortain Alps* by J.W. Akitt (pb Cicerone Press, 1995) - a guidebook for walkers which details 53 day-walks and four mostly short tours (including the *Tour des Glaciers de la Vanoise*) in these neighbouring mountain areas. Very useful for trekkers planning a return to explore the region further.

* *Walking the Alpine Parks of France & Northwest Italy* by Marcia R. Lieberman (pb The Mountaineers, Washington, 1994 - distributed in the UK by Cordée) - contains a chapter on the Vanoise National Park, with a number of day-walks and a few short tours described.

* *Walking the French Alps: GR5* by Martin Collins (pb Cicerone Press, 1984) - an excellent guide to this classic long-distance route. The book provides details of the GR55 trans-Vanoise stretch, as well as the main GR5 that crosses the region covered by the present guide (albeit in the opposite direction), and the Maurienne villages variant, GR5E.

* *Walking the GR5: Lake Geneva to Mont-Blanc* translated by Simon Knight (pb Robertson McCarta, 1990) - this is a direct translation from the French Topoguides produced by the Fédération Française de la Randonnée Pédestre (FFRP). The guide contains full-colour extracts from IGN maps, but in places the route is incorrectly marked. As with the Cicerone guide to the GR5 mentioned above, this particular book covers the Vanoise region well - GR55 and basic GR5 - but is now out of print.

* *Classic Walks of the World* edited by Walt Unsworth (pb Oxford Illustrated Press, 1985) - a large-format 'glossy' book which has a

chapter by Martin Collins describing the GR55 traverse of the Vanoise from Landry to Modane - nicely illustrated in colour and black & white. This book is now out of print, but may be ordered through local libraries.

* *The Outdoor Traveler's Guide: The Alps* by Marcia R. Lieberman (pb Stewart, Tabori & Chang, New York, 1991 - available from Stanfords in London) - lavishly illustrated with colour photographs by Tim Thompson, this is a good alpine primer by an American devotee to the Alps. A brief chapter is given to the Vanoise National Park.

*   *   *

APPENDIX D:
METRIC CONVERSIONS

1: Length:

To convert *to* metric, multiply by the factor shown. For conversions *from* metric, divide by the factor.

miles: kilometres	1.6093
yards: metres	0.9144
feet: metres	0.3048
inches: centimetres	2.54

Kilometres	Miles		Metres	Feet
0.5	0.3		100	328
1.0	0.6		300	984
1.6	1.0		500	1640
2.0	1.2		1000	3281
5.0	3.1		1500	4921
8.0	5.0		2000	6562
			2500	8202
			3000	9843
			3500	11483

2: Temperature:

To convert celcius to fahrenheit, divide by 5, then multiply the result by 9, and add 32.
To convert fahrenheit to celcius, subtract 32, divide the result by 9, and multiply by 5.

Celcius	Fahrenheit
0	32
10	50
20	68
30	86

3: Liquid Capacity:

To convert *to* metric, multiply by the factor given. To convert *from* metric, divide by the factor.

gallons: litres   4.546
pints: litres   0.568

Litres	Gallons		Litres	Pints
1	0.22		0.5	0.88
2	0.44		1	1.76
3	0.66		1.5	2.64
4	0.88		2	3.52
5	1.10		5	8.8

4: Weight:

To convert *to* metric, multiply by the factor shown. For conversions *from* metric, divide by the factor.

ounces: grams   28.3495
pounds: kilograms   0.4536

Grams	Ounces		Kilograms	Pounds
28.35	1		0.5	1.10
56.69	2		1	2.20
141.74	5		5	11
			10	22

*   *   *

APPENDIX E:
GLOSSARY

"One snag with France for the visitor," wrote Rob Hunter in his excellent *Walking in France*, "is that they do tend to speak rather a lot of French there!"

Whilst several refuge guardians and most staff at tourist information offices in the region speak some English, walkers following the Tour of the Vanoise will find that a few words of the French language will be very helpful. Besides (and I write this from a position of having an embarrassingly poor command of the language, even after 30-odd years of walking and climbing in French-speaking countries), it is an impertinence to expect the French to automatically speak English in their own country. Visitors should at least make an attempt to communicate a few words of French; the effort will be met with a willingness to understand. Hopefully the following list will be found useful.

English	*French*
accommodation	logement
bakery	boulangerie
bank	banque
bedroom	chambre
beer (draft beer)	bière (bière pression)
blister	ampoule
boots	chaussures de montagne
breakfast	petit déjeuner
bread	pain
bridge	pont
bus	autobus, autocar
bus station	gare routière
bus stop	arrêt autocar
butcher	boucher
cable-car	télépherique
cairn	cairn
campsite	le camping, terrain de camping
chairlift	télésiège
chamois	chamois
chapel	chapelle
chemist	pharmacie

church	église
closed	fermé
cloud	nuage
cold	froid
compass	boussole
crest (ridge)	crête
dam	barrage
dangerous	dangereux
dinner	dîner
dormitory	dortoir
eagle	aigle
east	est
easy	facile
exchange (currency)	échange
footpath	sentier, chemin
forbidden	défense de
forest	forêt
free	libre
full	complet
full board	pension complète
grocery	épicerie, alimentation
half-board (half-pension)	demi pension
help	secours
hill	colline
hotel list	liste d'hôtels
hour	heure
ibex	bouquetin
ice	glace
ice axe	piolet
information	information, renseignements
lake	lac
left (direction)	gauche
lightning	éclair
lunch	déjeuner
map	carte
marmot	marmotte
mountain	montagne
mountain hut	refuge
mountain inn	chalet-refuge
mountain stream	torrent
north	nord
occupied (toilet)	occupé
open	ouvert

outdoor activities	activités de plein air
pass	col
pasture	pâturage
railway	chemin de fer
railway station	gare
rain	pluie
reservoir	réservoir
ridge	arête
right (direction)	droit
room	chambre
rope	corde
rucksack	sac à dos
scree	éboulis
sheet sleeping bag	sac à viande
shelter	abri
shepherd's hut	bergerie
shop	magasin
shower	douche
sleeping bag	sac de couchage
snow	neige
south	sud
spring (of water)	source, fontaine
stonefall	chute de pierres
storm	tempête, orage
stream	ruisseau
sunny	ensoleillé, du soleil
sun stroke	coup de soleil
supermarket	supermarché
thunder	tonnerre
timetable	horaire
tourist office	office de tourisme, syndicat d'initiative
train	train
upper	dessous
valley	val, vallée
via, or over	via, par-dessus
warm	chaud
water	eau
waymark	balisage
weather forecast	météo
west	ouest
wind	vent
woodland	bois

* * *

PRINTED BY CARNMOR PRINT & DESIGN
95/97 LONDON ROAD, PRESTON, LANCASHIRE